DIET
SIGNS

DIET SIGNS

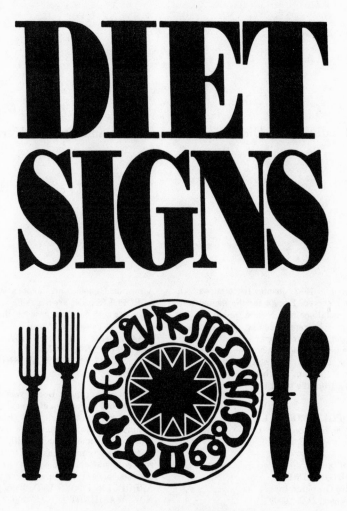

Joanne Lemieux

ACROPOLIS BOOKS LTD.

Dedicated to Dick and Suzie Lemieux and Anna P. Hero

ACROPOLIS BOOKS LTD.
Colortone Building, 2400 17th St., N.W., Washington, D.C. 20009

Printed in the United States of America by
COLORTONE PRESS
Creative Graphics, Inc.
Washington, D.C. 20009

Attention: Schools and Corporations
ACROPOLIS books are available at quantity discounts with bulk purchase for educational, business, or sales promotional use. For information, please write to: SPECIAL SALES DEPARTMENT, ACROPOLIS BOOKS LTD., 2400 17th ST., N.W., WASHINGTON, D.C. 20009

Are there Acropolis Books you want but cannot find in your local stores?
You can get any Acropolis book title in print. Simply send title and retail price, plus 50¢ per copy to cover mailing and handling costs for each book desired. District of Columbia residents add applicable sales tax. Enclose check or money order only, no cash please, to: ACROPOLIS BOOKS LTD., 2400 17th ST., N.W., WASHINGTON, D.C. 20009.

Library of Congress Cataloging in Publication Data

Lemieux, Joanne Hero, 1946-
   Diet signs.
   Bibliography: p.
   Includes index.
   1. Reducing diets.   2. Astrology and diet.
3. Reducing diets—Recipes.   4. Reducing exercise.
I. Title.
RM222.2.L4245   1982   613.2'5   82-16251
ISBN 0-87491-495-7 (pbk.)

Acknowledgments

For centuries, people have looked into the heavens for answers, and those who asked have found them.

All my love to Suzie and Dick Lemieux for their good humor and support at a time when I needed it.

My special thanks to the three people who encouraged me to share my research with others—Anna P. Hero, Frank V. Hero, and M. Antoinette Hero.

My sincerest gratitude to my assistant, Margaret Clandon-Cousins, who always knew we would do it.

My appreciation to my teachers—Valli Grimesey, Misty Kuceris, and Michael Munkasey.

To those people who unselfishly gave their support and first encouraged me to write—Donna Bellinger, Carole Jackson, Francine LaHue, Martha Martinez, Bonnie Uttech, and Dorothy Vitter—thank you. And especially to all the friends and neighbors who participated in the actual research.

Last, to the very special people—Al Hackl, Robert Hickey, Kathleen Hughes, and Laurie Tag who helped bring you this book.

Contents

Introduction

Before I wrote *Diet Signs* I was a four foot eleven inch astrologer who weighed 149 pounds. I had struggled through every diet you can imagine: nothing seemed to work for long. Then I noticed that there were times during the year that no matter how hard I tried, I lost nothing. At other times, it was easy to lose weight. Being an astrologer, I naturally started to chart these times. And then it hit me: they were really quite predictable astrological cycles!

The key to easy weight loss has been known for centuries, but until now it has been shrouded in mystery. It's a secret that most astrologers have overlooked or neglected to study. The secret to successful dieting is timing. For centuries astrologers and farmers have known that the sun affects the plumpness of fruits and vegetables, but now I've proved that it also affects the weight of people.

After I charted my own weight gain and loss cycles, I charted those of my clients in each sun sign. I then looked into the traditional foods, personality and eating traits for each sign. And, voilà, I came up with nutritious "sign-tailored" diets that will healthfully take the pounds off whenever followed, but work miracles when timed right. I've even been able to suggest an exercise program appropriate to the personality traits for each sign.

And it all works! My Cancer-tailored diet took an average of three and a half pounds off me every week. The weight loss was steady at times, dramatic at others; but I knew when these times would be and was never discouraged. I lost the thirty-five pounds I needed to lose in twelve weeks and have not had an irreversible weight gain since. My eating habits are "in tune with the stars."

But not only has *Diet Signs* worked for me, it's worked for every one of the clients to whom I've given it. Their reactions range from an Aquarius, who said, "With my busy schedule, I'm so glad I'm allowed a quick trip to a pizza parlor now and then, and stick to my diet." To a Scorpio, who raved, "I didn't diet, I just seemed to lose weight at the right time." And a Cancer who said, "The Cancer diet is really for me. Now I can lose weight easily."

Diet Signs takes the guesswork out of charting your own destiny and puts you back into the driver's seat of your life. Together we will explore why you overeat and how to overcome it. I have worked with a registered nurse to make the diets nutritionally sound. But be sure you check first with your doctor to be certain there is no medical reason for your being overweight. I've designed the menus to use food items normally found in your kitchen or grocery store. I've also devised delicious leftover dishes to save you money.

I'm always asked, "Do I have to wait until a certain time to start my diet?" The answer is, "No." You can start your diet whenever you feel the urge and do very well, but you may not see the dramatic weight loss that you will when your cycle is "right." The only rule of thumb is never, never start your diet before the full moon. Case in point, I was compelled by the transiting planet of discipline, Saturn, to begin my diet; but it was two weeks before the full moon. After two weeks of strict dieting, I only lost one pound, so I almost gave up. As soon as the full moon appeared, I lost five pounds overnight.

Believe me, I know that there is nothing more frustrating than being overweight in a diet-conscious society. But now, when you use your sign-tailored diet, you'll know exactly when you can lose the most weight with the least effort. You, too, will begin a self-confident journey to permanent weight loss "in tune with the stars."

Chapter 1

Is There A Diet In Your Horoscope?

Astrological dieting does work. It's worked for me and countless others. It will work for you.

Diet Signs will not teach you how to chart your horoscope, but it will teach you how to lose weight, healthfully and permanently through astrology.

Experts disagree as to what astrology is. Some say it is a science and some call it a religion. Astrologers themselves contend that the planets, sun and moon exert certain physical stresses on the earth. The effects of these stresses manifest themselves in weather patterns, plant and animal behavior, and, most notably, in ocean tides.

Astrology is not fortune telling. It cannot tell you what the future has in store for you. Astrology is the reading of your horoscope—the map of the planets at the time of your birth. Like any map, astrology can give you your boundaries and the obstacles you will encounter—in dieting, as well as in life. It will also show you how to use your cosmic energy by tapping into your strengths, and even your weaknesses, to overcome a certain obstacle—like being overweight.

Since the earth is constantly moving, nothing (including you) stays the same. To diet successfully, you must find out what your "givens" are—where the sun was in your chart when you were born, what sign was on the horizon (your rising sign), and the placement of the planets at the moment of your birth. The placement of your sun tells how you perceive the world and what motivates you. Your rising sign tells how the world perceives you. The placement of your moon reveals how you interpret this information. Don't worry, *Diet Signs* will teach you how to use these "givens" to lose weight.

Let's begin at the beginning, and your beginning is right now. If this is your first introduction to astrology, but not to dieting, you'll need to find your sun sign. First you must know what astrological sign the sun occupied on the day you were born—just look up your birth date and year on the Solar Position Chart in Appendix B. If you were born on the first or last three days of a sign, you are on a cusp. Since your sun takes on traits from both signs, read both descriptions in the following chapters and decide which diet will best suit you.

Now you are ready to begin your diet. Most diets limit your intake of all the things you love to eat, sometimes they do away with them altogether. Knowing that you must give up these foods, and accepting it, are two very different things. If you cannot live without coffee with cream and sugar, black coffee may not get you through even the first day of your diet. Many of us love and depend on certain foods, and the prospect of giving them up forever—or at least for the next ten to twenty pounds—may send us into fits of depression, or worse, into giving up the diet completely.

By recognizing the eating and personality traits for each sun sign, *Diet Signs* eliminates this formidable barrier to successful dieting forever. When you learn what your givens are, you can begin to work with them and not against them.

For instance, the fire signs (Aries, Leo and Sagittarius) have less trouble dieting than any other sun sign, since their bodies burn up calories most efficiently. Their diets are based on carbohydrate counting because their weakness stems from quantity: they will try to consume much more than they actually need, and they like foods with poor nutritional value. Their diets are based on the motto, "Eat like a queen in the morning, like a prince in the afternoon and like a beggar in the evening."

The earth signs, Taurus, Virgo and Capricorn, have a harder time losing weight because they let themselves gain weight for a long time before going on a diet.

The air signs, Gemini, Libra and Aquarius, have little trouble losing weight because they have so much nervous energy. They tend to go on way-out fad diets, however, and that's a weakness. They need to keep a diary of everything they eat in order to benefit from a diet.

The water signs, Cancer, Scorpio and Pisces, gain and lose weight at a phenomenal rate because most of their problem is not fat, but water weight.

Start your diet whenever the spirit—or the necessity—moves you. But remember that you will not see the dramatic results you crave unless you diet during the correct astrological cycles for your sign. Follow the simple formula for determining your best diet times, and stick to those. In other words, your dieting success depends on following the entire *Diet Signs* formula for your sign, including timing, eating patterns and preferences, and exercise.

Before you begin complete these four preliminary steps:

Step One: Self-Evaluation.
If you're reading this book, you want to lose weight. Check the Desirable Weight Chart in Appendix A and calculate how much weight you'd like to lose.

Step Two: Banish Guilt.

Realize there are times when you'll find it hard to lose weight. If you don't lose weight at these times, don't be hard on yourself. Think of those times when you've been bursting with willpower; then think of the other times when you would have killed for a cracker. We've all had times when we can seem to eat anything and still lose weight. Then there are times when you stick religiously to a diet and gain weight despite your efforts. Knowing your astrological cycles will help prepare you for those times.

Step Three: Timing is Everything.

Use your horoscope and learn to do the right thing, at the right place, at the right time. Jean Nidetch, the founder of Weight Watchers, is an example of someone with good timing. She had been overweight most of her life, but when she found the right place, the right people, and the right diet, she knew enough to take advantage of them.

Step Four: Know Yourself.

Everyone has a different reason for being overweight. Study your likes and dislikes. Get to know yourself. I *can* help you explore your astrological map, but only you can find the most direct route to your goal. *Diet Signs* will help you get there the fastest way possible—to lose the most weight with the least effort.

Aries

March 21-April 20   Day to start diet: Tuesday
Foods that govern sign: beef, onions, lamb, cranberries

Taurus

April 21-May 20   Day to start diet: Friday
Foods that govern sign: berries, cereal, wine

Gemini

May 21-June 20   Day to start diet: Wednesday
Foods that govern sign: above-ground vegetables, chicken

Cancer

June 21-July 20   Day to start diet: Monday
Foods that govern sign: shellfish, milk

Leo

July 21-August 20   Day to start diet: Sunday
Foods that govern sign: citrus fruits, cinnamon

Virgo

August 21-September 20   Day to start diet: Wednesday
Foods that govern sign: nuts, health food

Libra

September 21-October 20   Day to start diet: Friday
Foods that govern sign: tomatoes, mint, peaches

Scorpio

October 21-November 20   Day to start diet: Tuesday
Foods that govern sign: crustaceans, leftovers

Sagittarius

November 21-December 20   Day to start diet: Thursday
Foods that govern sign: bulb vegetables, outdoor cooking

Capricorn

December 21-January 20   Day to start diet: Saturday
Foods that govern sign: potatoes, spinach

Aquarius

January 21-February 20   Day to start diet: Saturday
Foods that govern sign: dried or frozen foods

Pisces

February 21-March 20   Day to start diet: Thursday
Foods that govern sign: cucumber, lettuce, melon, fish

Chapter 2

Diet Facts

All of our eating habits are learned. Many of us are overweight because we were given a cookie instead of love, candy instead of sympathy, and ice cream instead of a band-aid. And we remember what we learned as children. For many of us, food has come to symbolize love, appreciation, and affection. Food can literally make the hurt go away. But overeating in response to anxiety, stress, fatigue, and boredom can make us gain weight. And gaining weight can make many of us feel guilty.

After finishing *Diet Signs*, you will know your sun sign and be able to anticipate the times of year when you will be under solar stress. You will be attuned to those times when you're more likely to go off your diet or launch yourself on a binge. You will be able to take precautions—keeping high calorie foods out of the house or involving yourself in an activity that doesn't involve food. You will have more insight into yourself, learn why you overeat at certain times and not others, and what the danger signals are. If you should slip back into your old patterns, don't feel guilty. The cosmic stresses that caused you to overeat will pass quickly. Don't let yourself fall into the "What's the use?" trap. Your solar energy is there to draw on when you need it, so learn where your strengths lie and use them to achieve your purpose. Learn to like yourself. Appreciate your uniqueness.

Before starting the *Diet Signs* program, the most important thing to do, and I can't stress this enough, is check with your doctor to see if you need to diet. Make sure your weight problem isn't caused by disease or a chemical imbalance. There may be a very real *physical* reason you're overweight. This is especially likely if you've gained a lot of weight in a short time. Only after checking with your doctor should you proceed with your astrological diet.

The fire signs, Aries, Leo, and Sagittarius, have less of a problem dieting than the other signs because their bodies can burn up calories more efficiently. When the fire signs encounter weight problems, it's usually because they eat more than they actually need. Fire signs who live by the motto, "Eat like a queen in the morning, a prince in the afternoon, and a beggar in the evening," will probably never experience a problem with their weight.

Since fire signs do burn fuel efficiently, I advise a high protein/low carbohydrate diet. With the foods in their individualized menus, these natives can eat as much as they want as long as they don't exceed their daily limit of carbohydrates.

The earth signs, Taurus, Virgo, and Capricorn, have a harder time losing weight. This often results from letting too much time pass without dieting. According to one scientific theory, there are two kinds of fat: the first is used daily and burns off easily; the second, brown fat, is stored in the cells and not used until the first kind of fat is burned off. Consequently, brown fat is difficult to lose. Earth signs should be warned that the longer you keep it on, the harder it is to get off.

Since earth sign natives find losing weight hard, I've suggested a calorie-counting diet that sets a limit on how much they can eat. Keeping track of calories, as opposed to carbohydrates, makes it much easier for the weight-retaining earth signs not to eat more than they should.

The air signs, Gemini, Libra, and Aquarius, usually have little problem losing weight. Air sign natives always seem to be in high gear because they have so much nervous energy. Sticking to a diet and losing weight isn't much of a problem for air signs as long as they eat right and don't experiment with fad diets. Air signs should seriously consider using behavior modification techniques to help them diet. Keeping a food diary would be one useful diet tool.

Because air signs are nervous eaters, I've recommended a calorie-counting diet that includes three mini-meals each day. This diet allows air sign natives to eat continually, as they must do to maintain their high energy level, but it substitutes nutritional, low-calorie food for the junk food they usually snack on.

The water signs, Cancer, Scorpio, and Pisces, gain and lose weight at a phenomenal rate. Their problem isn't body fat, it's water retention. When the water signs do diet and lose, their weight loss may not register on the scale for as long as two weeks. As fat cells are depleted, the tissue around them absorbs water to replace the fat lost, and it can take up to two weeks for this process to occur. But once the tissues are flushed out, a dramatic weight loss should result.

This characteristic makes a calorie-counting diet that begins with a one-day liquid diet advisable. The fluid-retention problem that water signs are predisposed to makes a liquid diet essential. The day of liquids helps shrink the stomach and start the weight-loss process.

Every dieter's motto should be, "Lose weight any way you can without endangering your health or your life." Fad diets may or may not be detrimental to your health. They do take the pounds off quickly, but they don't produce a permanent change in your eating habits. You'll probably gain the weight back once you've gone off the diet.

Diet pills can be helpful in certain situations, but only if used under a doctor's supervision. Prolonged use of prescription or over-the-counter medications can be hazardous to your health. Amphetamines can be addictive, so exercise extreme caution when using any drugs, and discuss possible side effects with your doctor.

New research indicates that some people may be allergic to certain foods. A food allergy may cause a weight gain. It could interfere with the impulses to the brain that tell you when you're full. Because of this interference, someone with a food allergy may continue to eat even when they're no longer hungry. Have you ever felt uncomfortably full yet continued eating? You may have a food allergy, and any food could be the trigger that sets off your reaction.

There are substances in certain foods that are addictive. The caffeine in coffee and chocolate can be addictive. You can't seem to live without these foods because your body has come to depend on them. Satisfying an addiction can be a time-consuming preoccupation. Are there foods in your life that you crave and are irritable without? If the answer is yes, then you're probably addicted. Cut out this food and you'll lose weight, but giving up your addiction is easier said than done. When you give up your addiction, you may suffer withdrawal pains. The first couple of days are the worst. You may feel irritable, depressed, and tired. The fatigued feeling may last for a couple of weeks, but the craving should begin to subside and at the end of about three weeks, you should see a marked improvement in your health. If you get through this, dieting will be a cinch.

I have outlined different techniques for cutting down your calorie or carbohydrate intake. Since none of these techniques will work for everyone, I've tried to include only those that have successfully curbed the appetites of most of those people I interviewed.

- Fast foods do *not* make you overweight, especially if you know their calorie or carbohydrate count. Choose wisely and eat and drink in moderation.

- By reducing your calorie or carbohydrate intake, you will reduce your weight. Use less cooking oil; stir-fry instead of deep fat frying; broil, poach, or steam most of your foods; use less butter. Be inventive, experiment with different spices. Use lemon or lime juice, low calorie dressings and sauces.

- The less time you spend with food, the less chance you will have to eat. The more you come in contact with food, the more likely you are to revert to your old eating habits.

- Knowing that your favorite foods are high in calories or carbohydrates doesn't mean you have to cut it out of your diet. It does mean that you will know the amount you can have without exceeding your daily allotment. Incorporate your favorite foods into your diet sensibly.

- Think in terms of quality, not quantity. This will enable you to cut calories or carbohydrates and add nutritional value to your diet.

- By adding a soup or salad course before your entree, you'll feel less hungry and, therefore, won't eat as much.

- If you can pinpoint *why* you overeat—anxiety, stress, boredom, anger, fatigue, addiction, allergies—you will have the tools to control your appetite.

- There are some marvelous prepackaged low calorie meals now on the market (e.g., Weight Watcher meals and Lean Cuisine). For a simple, delicious meal without the trouble of counting calories eat it as is or add a salad and a low calorie drink.

- Most of us reward ourselves with food. By breaking this habit, you can cut down on your food intake. Instead of food, reward yourself with something non-fattening—shoes, a new dress, a good movie.

- By setting more realistic goals for ourselves, we are more apt to stick with them. Break down your ultimate goal into equal parts. For example, when you've lost one-third of your goal, change your makeup to show off the new you. It's fun to let a department store beauty consultant make you over. In most big cities, there is no charge for this service. Upon reaching the two-thirds mark, have your hair restyled. After you reach your goal, buy some new clothes, and then wait for all the compliments that will come your way.

- If you select a diet plan you and your family can live with, you won't have any trouble adapting to your new eating habits. Always try to serve your family the same things you eat. This cuts down on preparation time, saves time and money, and reduces the likelihood that you'll go off your diet.

- It may be difficult for you to lose weight because of your lifestyle, society, family, or friends. They may, unintentionally or intentionally, sabotage your efforts to diet. You may be made to feel guilty if you leave food on your plate, or you may have a mother who thinks you are too skinny and gives you enough food to keep the 10th Battalion in rations for a week! If you don't eat it, then you get the, "what's a mother to do, you cook, you clean, you slave and for what?" routine. Get the picture? If you can't get support at home, groups like Weight Watchers or Overeaters Anonymous can really help. People in these organizations are understanding and sympathetic. They can counsel you on how to handle those situations and people who are undermining your diet. Diet Centers will work with you on an individual basis to help solve your weight problems.

- Diet pills *can* be addictive if not taken according to a doctor's directions.

- Fad diets can be harmful to your health. Be sure your diet is safe. Always check with your doctor if you have any questions.

- If you lose weight too quickly, the resulting drop in your blood sugar level can cause headaches and nausea. Your body is trying to tell you something. Do everything in moderation.

- You can *do* the things you fantasize about while you are dieting. Being slim doesn't make your dreams come true. Only *you* can turn your fantasies into realities. The time to make your grand entrance is *now*.

Chapter 3

Aries

Aries, symbolized by the Ram and ruled by the planet Mars, is the first sign in the zodiac. Aries is the cosmic beginning, not unlike a gallant leader who pioneers the way for the less adventurous. If you're an Aries, you enjoy being first. You are always out in front of everyone, and that is where you belong. How does this relate to your ability to diet? Because you are a fire sign, you find it easier to lose weight than any other sign in the zodiac. But if you were born in the last ten days of your sun sign, you will have more of a problem dieting than the typical Aries.

You are blessed with a sparkling personality and a sunny disposition. People love to be with you, and you enjoy the company of others. Many people envy the childlike enthusiasm you bring to everything you do. Many of us wish we could embrace life as impetuously as you do. But that same impetuousness can sometimes lead you down some strange paths. The Aries native acts first and considers the consequences later. Although you would never intentionally hurt someone, your blunt Aries approach can have that effect, much to your dismay. Your quick smile, your wit, and your engaging personality will smooth things over and get you off the hook.

You are viewed as a maverick because you dare to be different. Keeping a low profile is not your style, and what style you have. You can always be counted on to do the unusual. Your originality always surprises and delights your fans and friends. You have more than your share of energy, and there is nothing you can't accomplish if you set your mind to it. Aries are at their best when faced with new mental and physical challenges.

Aries are quick, exciting, mobile, high-spirited, independent. You are always searching, always looking for new worlds to conquer. It's hard for the rest of us to keep up with you.

Your health is basically good. You have a sound constitution, but you are high-strung, like most other thoroughbreds. Some people might describe you as temperamental, especially when you don't get your way. Try to be more patient. Realize that things take time. But sometimes that temper of yours works to your advantage. When all else fails, your determination to succeed will keep you on your diet.

You see yourself in terms of what you accomplish on your own, without help from anyone else. You live for the challenge, you thrive on competition, and you get great satisfaction from winning. You don't like being just "one of the boys or girls." You need to be a winner. And that's wonderful because you know you are the best. Once you know what you want, you make it happen.

For an Aries, the most difficult part of a diet is sticking with it. You are great at beginnings, but you rapidly lose interest. If you can't visualize your goal or if you can't achieve your goal quickly, you give up and want to move on to other challenges. People who aren't familiar with this Aries characteristic might think that you don't finish what you start. But anyone who knows you, knows that isn't the case. It's not that you've abandoned your original goals, instead you've gained new insight into yourself and your motives. In this way, new goals have evolved and your old goals are obsolete.

You enjoy entertaining and are considered a good host. Your guests leave raving about the decor, the food, and the company. You manage to make it all look simple. You are usually a good cook, and, if you aren't, you know the best caterer in town. You would like hot, spicy food. Limiting, monotonous diets aren't for you. You need as much variety in your diet as you do in your life. The more exotic the food, the better you like it. Finding a well-balanced diet that includes the hot, spicy, exotic food you like is difficult, but not impossible. Whatever diet you decide on, make sure that it won't deplete your energy. Patience is not one of your virtues, so pay particular attention to those diets that will help you lose weight quickly.

Astrology will help you pinpoint the times when losing weight will be quite easy. It will also show you when you will be less successful. These times will pass quickly. But since in times like these we tend to go off our diets, recognize that these cosmic stresses won't last forever. They may last an hour, a day, or a month, but never longer. When these stresses have passed, you can resume your diet and successfully lose weight.

Aries seldom get fat because their bodies usually burn calories efficiently. Problems can arise from one of two sources. You tend to eat too fast, which means your stomach doesn't have a chance to tell your brain that you've eaten enough. Slow down. Enjoy a nice, leisurely meal for a change. You also prefer snacking to eating three meals a day. Eating on the run is fine occasionally, but snacks usually contain empty calories. The real problem is boredom. When you're bored, you eat. You often don't realize how much you've actually eaten. This, coupled with your tendency to eat too fast, takes its toll on you and your body.

Aries is ruled by the planet Mars, the energizer and the God of War. Since Mars is supposed to have smiled on those who asked favors from him on Tuesdays, you should begin dieting on the Tuesday after the full moon. The moon influences how much fluid we will retain. No matter when you start your diet, you will lose pounds, but you will see little actual weight loss until the moon wanes. When the sun enters Aries (March 21-April 20) or Leo (July 21-August 20), you will experience a dramatic weight loss and decrease in your appetite. But you will gain it all back if you don't stick to a maintenance diet. You may find it harder to lose weight when the sun enters Cancer (June 21-July 20) or when the sun moves into your second house, Taurus (April 21-May 20). To ensure success, begin your diet in early spring or late summer. You will also find it easier to maintain your weight loss during these periods.

The Aries native finds it hard to appreciate the progress they've already made. Have patience. Aim to lose ten pounds at first, regardless of how much you want to lose. Then take time out to enjoy your success and, at this same time, try out a maintenance diet.

It is easy for an Aries to burn calories, but, in order to do this, you have to exercise. You need plenty of fresh air and sunshine. The more you exercise, the less you have to diet.

Janine, a slim, glamorous Aries from Switzerland, is a terrific example of someone who listens to the signals her body gives her. As one of the leading cosmetic consultants in the San Francisco Bay area, Janine wants to look her best at all times. Like most Aries, Janine has less of a weight problem than most of the other sun signs, but once a year she experiences a large weight gain. I asked Janine how she managed to maintain her beautiful figure. Her secret: exercise, exercise, and more exercise. Janine prefers the excitement of an outdoor, competitive sport. She finds that exercise not only helps her lose weight, it also does wonders for her complexion and her mental health.

Most Aries natives resemble Janine in that they do not like exercising alone. Since you are people-oriented, find an activity that involves other people. Join a health spa, take up tennis, or learn to play racquetball. Whatever sports you decide on, go slowly at first. You tend to overdo anything you're enthusiastic about. Pace yourself so you don't suffer from exhaustion or muscle strain. Find a friend who doesn't mind losing, because once you've mastered your chosen sport, you'll be a winner.

The charts on the following pages will help you find the best time for *you* to lose weight. The easy-to-use astrological wheel has directions on setting up your chart by using your birthday. It shows you how to follow your sun's progress through your twelve houses. The Solar Transit Chart lets you record your weight loss as the sun moves from one house to the next. There is also a first week's menu that will allow you to include the foods you and your family love in your diet.

Familiarize yourself with the astrological wheel and the significance of each house as it pertains to the Aries native. The houses follow in a counterclockwise circle. Each house covers about a thirty-day period.

- When the Aries sun transits your first house (Aries), you want to enhance your appearance (weight loss).

- When the Aries sun transits your second house (Taurus), you want to indulge yourself (weight gain).

- When the Aries sun transits your third house (Gemini), you are better able to express your ideas.

- When the Aries sun transits your fourth house (Cancer) you want to nurture yourself (weight gain).

- When the Aries sun transits your fifth house (Leo), you achieve more confidence in yourself, your appearance, and your abilities (weight loss).

- When the Aries sun transits your sixth house (Virgo), you become more interested in your health and working conditions.

- When the Aries sun transits your seventh house (Libra), you form new relationships and your interest in other people is renewed.

- When the Aries sun transits your eighth house (Scorpio), you become more interested in the resources of others as they affect you.

- When the Aries sun transits your ninth house (Sagittarius), you devise new plans for the future.

- When the Aries sun transits your tenth house (Capricorn), you move ahead with your career plans.

- When the Aries sun transits your eleventh house (Aquarius), you want to cooperate with others in a group effort.

- When the Aries sun transits your twelfth house (Pisces), you discover information previously unavailable to you.

- As the sun leaves your twelfth house and prepares to enter your first house again, you will have a chance to reassess your last solar year and make plans for the year ahead.

To personalize the Aries solar wheel, insert your birthdate in the blank space marked number 1 Aries. Then moving counterclockwise, insert the next month and same day in the blank space marked number 2 Taurus. Continue around the solar wheel, marking the month and day in the blank spaces, until you come full circle.

You will now be able to follow the sun's transits through your horoscope and anticipate what aspects of your life will be highlighted each thirty-day period. The transits will also tell you the times during the year you can diet most successfully. For those people born on the cusp of a sign (three days before or three days after) refer to the Solar Position Chart to find out what your sun sign really is.

Sample Solar Wheel

for Al H.   Birthday: March 31

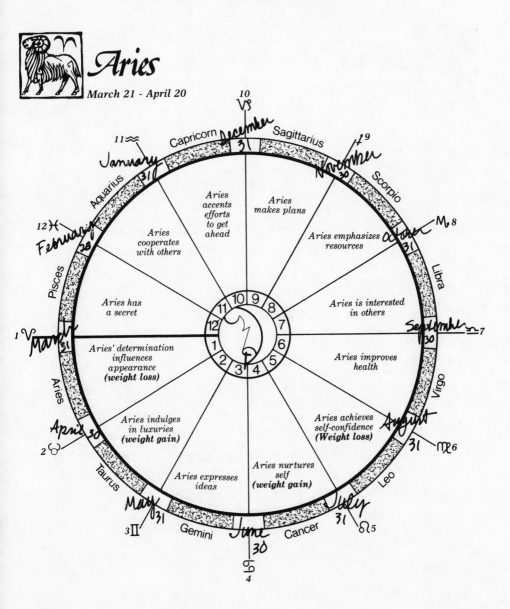

Aries

March 21 - April 20

Solar Wheel Chart

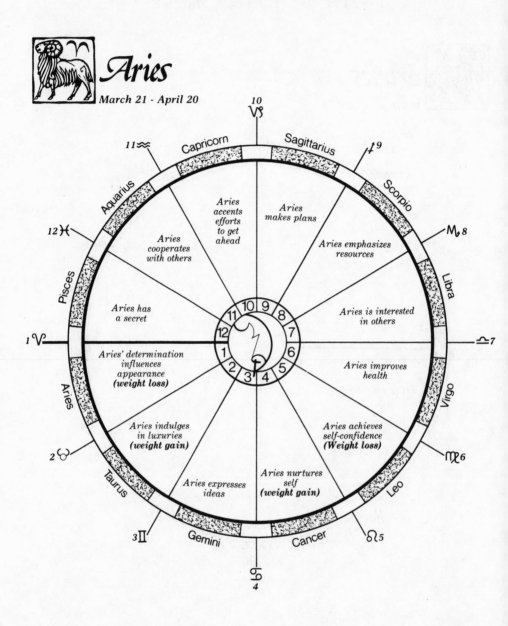

Aries

March 21 - April 20

10 ♑

11 ♒ Capricorn   Sagittarius ♐ 9

Aquarius   Scorpio

12 ♓   ♏ 8

Pisces   Libra

Aries accents efforts to get ahead

Aries makes plans

Aries cooperates with others

Aries emphasizes resources

Aries has a secret

Aries is interested in others

1 ♈   ♎ 7

Aries' determination influences appearance **(weight loss)**

Aries improves health

Aries   Virgo

Aries indulges in luxuries **(weight gain)**

Aries achieves self-confidence **(Weight loss)**

2 ♉   ♍ 6

Taurus   *Aries expresses ideas*   *Aries nurtures self* **(weight gain)**   Leo

3 ♊ Gemini   Cancer   ♌ 5

♋ 4

The Solar Transit Chart provides you with a guide to those times of the year when you will lose weight and those times you will gain weight.

Insert your birth date at the top of the chart in the space marked number 1 Aries. Then insert the next month and same day in the space marked number 2 Taurus. Continue across the top of the page until you reach 12 Pisces.

Record your total weight loss or gain with an X. (See the example). At the end of the solar year, connect the Xs to reveal your astrological pattern.

Sample Solar Transit Chart

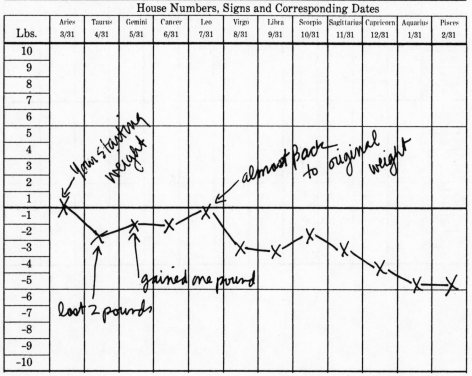

Lbs.	Aries 3/31	Taurus 4/31	Gemini 5/31	Cancer 6/31	Leo 7/31	Virgo 8/31	Libra 9/31	Scorpio 10/31	Sagittarius 11/31	Capricorn 12/31	Aquarius 1/31	Pisces 2/31
10												
9												
8												
7												
6												
5												
4												
3												
2												
1												
-1												
-2												
-3												
-4												
-5												
-6												
-7												
-8												
-9												
-10												

Caption text on chart: Your starting weight — gained one pound — lost 2 pounds — almost back to original weight

Aries Solar Transit Chart

House Numbers, Signs and Corresponding Dates

Lbs.	Aries	Taurus	Gemini	Cancer	Leo	Virgo	Libra	Scorpio	Sagittarius	Capricorn	Aquarius	Pisces
10												
9												
8												
7												
6												
5												
4												
3												
2												
1												
−1												
−2												
−3												
−4												
−5												
−6												
−7												
−8												
−9												
−10												

When you begin contemplating your diet, look seriously at the high protein/low carbohydrate diets. Try to incorporate all of the red meats, fruits and vegetables and drink at least eight glasses of water daily.

The following diet is high in protein and low in carbohydrates. It includes many of the foods an Aries loves. You are allowed 60 grams of carbohydrates a day. Check any substitutions with the calorie/carbohydrate/protein counter in Appendix C. Recipes for some of the dishes (marked with an asterisk) in your diet plan appear in Chapter 15.

Aries: First Week's Menu

Day One: Tuesday

BREAKFAST   Carbohydrates (in grams)
fried eggs in butter (unlimited amount) ..   1
1 slice of protein toast with butter........   9
6 oz. V-8 juice..........................   7
coffee or tea (with/without heavy cream) .   0-1

LUNCH
hamburger patty (unlimited amount).....   1
lettuce and tomato salad (use dressing
    sparingly)   6
iced tea, coffee, diet soda, water..........   0-1

DINNER
broccoli beef*   8
½ c. rice   21
½ c. strawberries with heavy cream   6
1 glass dry red wine (claret, burgundy) ..   1
coffee or tea (with/without heavy cream) .   0-1
                                         _____
                                          60-63

Day Two: Wednesday

BREAKFAST   Carbohydrates (in grams)
plain yogurt with fresh, unsweetened fruit
    and 1 tsp. wheat germ.................   29
coffee or tea (with/without heavy cream) .   0-1

LUNCH
chicken bouillon........................ 0
chef salad(use dressing sparingly)........ 6
2 saltines 4
iced tea, coffee, diet soda, water.......... 0-1

DINNER
meat loaf, no filler (unlimited
   amount) 1
boiled potatoes 12
green beans in butter with slivered
   almonds 6
1 glass dry red wine (claret, burgundy) .. 1
coffee or tea (with/without heavy cream) . 0-1

TOTAL   59-62

Day Three: Thursday

BREAKFAST
Carbohydrates (in grams)
6 oz. orange juice....................... 8
hard-boiled eggs (unlimited amount) 1
piece of cheddar or hard cheese 1
coffee or tea (with/without heavy cream) . 0-1

LUNCH
tuna salad 3
cherry tomatoes 4
4 Ritz crackers......................... 8
iced tea, coffee, diet soda, water.......... 0-1

DINNER
lamb curry with rice* 18
salad with lettuce, tomato, grated
   cheddar cheese 6
1 glass dry red wine (claret, burgundy) .. 1
coffee or tea (with/without heavy cream) . 0-1

TOTAL   50-53

Day Four: Friday

BREAKFAST
Carbohydrates (in grams)
6 oz. V-8 juice......................... 7
1 bran muffin with butter and/or cream
   cheese............................... 15
coffee or tea (with/without heavy cream) . 0-1

LUNCH

2 tacos or egg salad sandwich on protein
    bread 18
carrot sticks 5
iced tea, coffee, diet soda, water.......... 0-1

DINNER

fish cooked in butter (unlimited amount) . 1
broccoli and cheese sauce 5
lettuce wedge sprinkled with grated cheese
    and chopped hard-boiled egg (blue
    cheese or oil and vinegar dressing)..... 4
1 glass dry white wine (chablis, Rhine) ... 1
coffee or tea (with/without heavy cream) . 0-1

Total   56-59

Day Five: Saturday

BRUNCH   Carbohydrates (in grams)

1 c. cottage cheese...................... 5
fresh fruit salad........................ 21
1 slice protein toast with butter 9
coffee or tea (with/without heavy cream) . 0-1

DINNER

steak (unlimited amount) 1
mushrooms in butter 3
spinach salad with bacon bits 5
¼ c. vanilla ice cream with one shot of
    creme de menthe or creme de cacao ... 14
1 glass dry red wine (claret, burgundy) .. 1
coffee or tea (with/without heavy cream) . 0-1

Total   58-61

Day Six: Sunday

BRUNCH   Carbohydrates (in grams)

8 oz. V-8 juice.......................... 9
2 chicken in the basket (two slices protein
    bread and two eggs) 18
Canadian bacon (unlimited amount)...... 0
coffee or tea (with/without heavy cream) . 0-1

DINNER

turkey au jus (unlimited amount)	1
½ c. mashed potatoes	14
asparagus (with butter or hollandaise sauce)	4
fresh strawberries in champagne	8
1 glass dry white wine (chablis, Rhine) ...	1
coffee or tea (with/without heavy cream) .	0-1
Total	55-57

Day Seven: Monday

BREAKFAST   Carbohydrates (in grams)

6 oz. grapefruit juice	18
1 c. Kellogg's *Special K* cereal	7
¼ c. light cream, 1 tsp. sugar	5
coffee or tea (with/without heavy cream) .	0-1

LUNCH

beef noodle soup.........................	5
chicken salad	2
iced tea, coffee, diet soda, water..........	0-1

DINNER

martini or scotch on the rocks............	1
chili*	9
one slice cheddar cheese	1
avocado, lettuce, and tomato salad (use dressing sparingly)	5
coffee or tea (with/without heavy cream) .	0-1
Total	53-56

Chapter 4

Taurus

Taurus, the first earth sign in the zodiac, is symbolized by the bull. You are ruled by the planet Venus and carry the weight of the second house. Taurus represents the good things of life—wealth, material possessions, financial security. You are the strongest sign in the zodiac. This quiet inner strength of yours makes you able to hold fast when others would give up. Once you've set your course of action, nothing can stop you from achieving your goal. This singlemindedness will help you diet.

The Taurus native does not make close friends easily, and those you do have are highly prized. For you, friendships should last a lifetime. Your friends find you loyal, trustworthy, and feel lucky to have known you.

You appear to take your own sweet time when given a new task. Some people find this trait exasperating. But there is nothing slow about you. You want to analyze all the facts before you act. You need to look at a problem from all possible angles, and then study every detail you unearth. The Taurus native never leaves anything to chance—either you do it right the first time or you don't do it at all. The Taurean motto is, "Look before you leap." Aries is the pioneer; Taurus, the builder. You take great pride in everything you do. Whatever you build, you build it to last.

Patience is one of your greatest virtues, and it takes a lot to make you angry. But there are some things even Taurus won't put up with. Once angered, you become a raging Taurus bull. You will go to great lengths to keep the peace, but people cannot take advantage of your good nature all the time. You have no trouble telling someone they've pushed you too far.

Earth and fixed signs are usually conservative. They dislike change. Taurus natives like the tried and true method of doing things. You feel more comfortable with the familiar, so try to be a little more flexible. By being more flexible, you may achieve the emotional and financial security that is so important to you. Your life is well organized. You prefer doing things according to a routine, and you feel in control only if you know what will happen next. When you're forced to change, you may feel out of control. For you, security means being in control. So how does this affect your ability to diet?

Dieting does not come easily for you. Taurean men and women appreciate and enjoy fine food. Most foods you do like are loaded with calories, and it's hard for you to refuse the foods you love. Most Taurus natives have a mealtime routine, and any change in that routine can be upsetting.

Venus, your ruling planet, has given you an appetite for the finer things in life—art, music, good food, and fine wines. Venus, the goddess of love, confers great beauty on those born under her influence. But, her idea of beauty and that which we today call beauty are two different things. This difference is quite dramatic if you compare the beautiful men and women of Venus's time with that of more contemporary men and women. You will notice that earlier beauties were well-endowed, whereas today, we know that excess weight can cause serious health problems. Besides being well-endowed and an appreciator of the finer things in life, Venus has bestowed you with a charismatic personality that attracts members of the opposite sex. She has also given you sex appeal that won't quit and she's taught you how to use it.

Frances is an example of a sexy Taurus. I've never quite figured out what she has or how she got it, but when Frances enters a room every man in the place turns around to stare at her. But as sexy as she is, Frances is always fighting the battle of the bulge. She would love to know when to start a diet that would work immediately. So I charted her horoscope, and three weeks ago Frances's Taurus sun entered her first house and she began to diet. She has lost eight pounds so far, and, with true Taurean determination, she continues to lose.

Taurean natives like Frances are gifted with strength of purpose unequaled by any of the other signs. With this will-power, nothing can stop you from achieving your goals. You can overcome any obstacle in your path. You can refuse that hot fudge sundae and pass up that piece of pecan pie when lesser mortals would falter. You indulge yourself where food is concerned. You eat only the best foods; you won't settle for less.

You come by your large appetite and robust physique naturally. Problems arise when you begin to eat empty calories. These empty calories only add pounds, sap your strength and energy, and make it hard for you to burn off that excess fat efficiently. Don't feel that you'll have to give up all those foods that you enjoy to lose weight. But you should cut back on how much you eat. You'll have to change the self-destructive eating habits you've established over the years, but Taurean determination gives you the willpower you'll need. Start now to cut down, not cut out, all the foods you love to eat. This may mean lighter meals than you're used to and smaller portions than you'd like, but stick with it.

Try cutting back on candy, cakes, cookies, crackers, chips, ice cream, soft drinks, and alcoholic beverages. No more second helpings of dessert (don't cheat by taking one large one). This doesn't mean you have to give up desserts for good, just try some substitutes. Instead of cake, eat fresh fruit; instead of soft drinks, try juice, herb tea, or mineral water;

instead of a handful of potato chips, try a handful of vegetables or a cup of lightly salted popcorn. Instead of a martini try a light beer or a glass of dry white wine.

Astrology won't give you the willpower to stay on a diet—you were born with it. But astrology will identify those times when losing weight will be easier for you. Times when losing weight is difficult, despite conscientious dieting, will pass quickly. You are more likely to stray from your diet during times of cosmic stress. Don't feel guilty if that happens. When the stress has passed, resume your diet. Don't worry about what or how much you ate. Start back where you left off. You'll lose weight quickly if you haven't gained too much.

The Taurus native should always begin his or her diet on a Friday. Start your diet on a Friday, and, on the following Friday reward yourself for sticking to your diet. Your reward doesn't have to be food, but if it is, breathe in its aroma, savor every mouthful, remind yourself what you like about that particular food. When it is all gone, go back on your diet until the following Friday.

There are several times during the astrological year when you'll get the best results from your diet. When the sun enters your first house, or just after your birthday; then when the sun enters your fifth house, Virgo (August 21-September 20), or during the last few days of summer. You'll be amazed at how easy it is to lose weight during those times. You'll wonder why you had such difficulties before. Do not begin your diet when the sun is in Gemini (May 21-June 20) or Leo (July 21-August 20). At these two times of the year, you'll find it easier to maintain your weight but harder to lose it. Never begin your diet until after the full moon.

You alone must decide you want to lose weight. Check with your doctor first to rule out any physiological or metabolic problems. If everything checks out, ask your doctor to help you set a realistic goal. Once you have made this commitment, nothing will stand in your way. Taureans cannot be forced to do anything they don't want to do. You know what's right for you. If a diet is right for you, then you'll go on a diet.

Everyone who is on a diet needs encouragement and support. Tell your family and close friends you are dieting and that it's important to you. They'll help you in any way they can. You can also find many diet support groups and diet clinics staffed with trained professionals who know and understand your problem. Look in the yellow pages under "Reducing and Weight Control Services."

Many diet clubs and reducing clinics stress diet over exercise. You will feel better if you exercised, but it isn't one of your stronger points. Begin to incorporate exercise into your daily routine. The Tauras native has great strength but less energy than some of the more active signs.

The best way for you to get your body back into shape is by developing good eating habits—fewer calories and more exercise. Light exercise is fun and will get you moving. Take up dancing lessons or find a partner and go dancing. Most Taureans are excellent dancers and, no matter how much weight they gain, are always light on their feet. If you don't know how to dance, look around and Venus will provide you with a partner who does.

The charts on the following pages will help you find the best time for *you* to lose weight. The easy-to-use astrological wheel has directions on setting up your chart by using your birthday. It shows you how to follow your sun's progress through your twelve houses. The Solar Transit Chart lets you record your weight loss as the sun moves from one house to the next. There is also a first week's menu that will allow you to include the foods you and your family love in your diet.

Familiarize yourself with the astrological wheel and the significance of each house as it pertains to the Taurus native. The houses follow in a counterclockwise circle. Each house covers about a thirty-day period.

- When the Taurus sun transits your first house (Taurus), you want to enhance your appearance (weight loss).

- When the Taurus sun transits your second house (Gemini), you want to indulge yourself (weight gain).

- When the Taurus sun transits your third house (Cancer), you are better able to express your ideas.

- When the Taurus sun transits your fourth house (Leo), you want to nurture yourself.

- When the Taurus sun transits your fifth house (Virgo), you achieve more confidence in yourself, your appearance, and your abilities (weight loss).

- When the Taurus sun transits your sixth house (Libra), you become more interested in your health and working conditions.

- When the Taurus sun transits your seventh house (Scorpio), you form new relationships and your interest in other people is renewed.

- When the Taurus sun transits your eighth house (Sagittarius), you become more interested in the resources of others as they affect you.

- When the Taurus sun transits your ninth house (Capricorn), you devise new plans for the future.

- When the Taurus sun transits your tenth house (Aquarius), you want to move ahead with your career plans.

- When the Taurus sun transits your eleventh house (Pisces), you want to cooperate in a group effort.

- When the Taurus sun transits your twelfth house (Aries), you discover information previously unavailable to you.

• As the sun leaves your twelfth house and prepares to enter your first house again, you will be given a chance to reassess your last solar year and lay plans for the new year ahead.

To personalize the Taurus solar wheel, insert your birthdate in the blank space marked number 1 Taurus. Then moving counter-clockwise, insert the next month and same day in the blank space marked number 2 Gemini. Continue around the solar wheel, marking the month and day in the blank spaces, until you come full circle.

You will now be able to follow the sun's transits through your horoscope and anticipate what aspects of your life will be highlighted each thirty-day period. The transits will also tell you the times during the year you can diet most successfully. For those people born on the cusp of a sign (three days before or three days after) refer to the Solar Position Chart to find out what your sun sign really is.

To see how one dieter personalized his solar wheel, see page 29.

Solar Wheel Chart

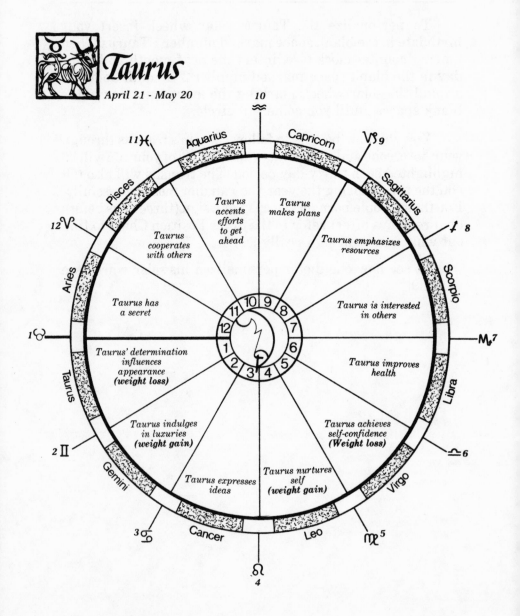

Taurus

April 21 - May 20

Aquarius — 11 ♓

Capricorn — ♒ 10

Pisces — ♑ 9 — Sagittarius

Aries — 12 ♈ — ♐ 8 — Scorpio

Taurus — 1 ♉ — ♏ 7

Gemini — 2 ♊ — ♎ 6 — Libra — Virgo

Cancer — 3 ♋ — ♍ 5 — Leo

♌ 4

Taurus accents efforts to get ahead

Taurus makes plans

Taurus cooperates with others

Taurus emphasizes resources

Taurus has a secret

Taurus is interested in others

Taurus' determination influences appearance *(weight loss)*

Taurus improves health

Taurus indulges in luxuries *(weight gain)*

Taurus achieves self-confidence *(Weight loss)*

Taurus expresses ideas

Taurus nurtures self *(weight gain)*

The Solar Transit Chart provides you with a guide to those times of the year when you will lose weight and those times you will gain weight.

Insert your birthdate at the top of the chart in the space marked number 1 Taurus. Then insert the next month and same day in the space marked number 2 Gemini. Continue across the top of the page until you reach 12 Aries.

Record your total weight loss or gain with an X. At the end of the solar year, connect the Xs to reveal your astrological pattern.

To see how one dieter recorded her weight, see page 31.

Taurus Solar Transit Chart

House Numbers, Signs and Corresponding Dates

Lbs.	Taurus	Gemini	Cancer	Leo	Virgo	Libra	Scorpio	Sagittarius	Capricorn	Aquarius	Pisces	Aries
10												
9												
8												
7												
6												
5												
4												
3												
2												
1												
–1												
–2												
–3												
–4												
–5												
–6												
–7												
–8												
–9												
–10												

I've outlined a week's worth of menus. Women are allotted 1200 calories, men 1500 calories. Never skip breakfast. If you like, it can be your biggest meal of the day. Make lunch and dinner lighter meals. Try not to deviate too much from your normal routine. Eat the same foods, at the same time, in the same place—just change how much. Check the calorie/carbohydrate/protein counter in Appendix C before substituting or exchanging foods. Recipes for some of the dishes (marked with an asterisk) in your diet plan appear in Chapter 15.

Taurus: First Week's Menu

Day One: Friday

BREAKFAST   Calories
yogurt shake* 135
1 egg, cooked any way 100
1 slice toast with 1 pat butter 106
1 cup coffee or tea (with/without skim milk
    and 1 tsp. sugar) 0-25

LUNCH
½ c. tuna salad 280
lettuce leaf.............................. 5
1 dill pickle 10
1 cup coffee or tea with/without skim milk
    and 1 tsp. sugar), diet soda, water 0-25

DINNER
cube steak with peppers and tomato* 260
lettuce and tomato salad (1 tbsp. diet
    dressing) 60
dessert peaches.......................... 50
1 glass light beer 80
1 cup coffee or tea (with/without skim milk
    and 1 tsp. sugar), diet soda, water 0-25

Total   1086-
1161

Day Two: Saturday

BREAKFAST   Calories
1 c. vegetable juice 40
1 vegetable omelette 260-
                                          360
1 cup coffee or tea (with/without skim milk
    and 1 tsp. sugar)..................... 0-25

LUNCH
4 oz. steamed shrimp on lettuce 108
1 c. Manhattan clam chowder............ 81
1 apple 61
1 cup coffee or tea (with/without skim milk
    and 1 tsp. sugar), diet soda, water 0-25

DINNER
½ 10" cheese pizza...................... 500
salad with 1 tbsp. diet dressing 60
1 glass light beer, diet soda, water 0-80

                              Total   1110-
                                       1340

Day Three: Sunday

BREAKFAST   Calories
1 serving eggs benedict.................. 296
fruit salad 126
1 cup coffee or tea (with/without skim milk
    and 1 tsp. sugar)..................... 0-25

LUNCH
1 lb. lobster with 1 tbsp. butter 212
4 oz. steak 235
½ baked potato with 1 pat butter (or 1 tbsp.
    sour cream and chives)............... 111
salad with 1 tbsp. diet dressing 60
1 glass wine, diet soda, water 0-90
1 cup coffee or tea (with/without skim milk
    and 1 tsp. sugar)..................... 0-25

DINNER

1 open-face melted cheese sandwich with tomato	185
½ c. tomato soup	55
1 cup coffee or tea (with/without skim milk and 1 tsp. sugar), diet soda, water	0-25
Total	1280-1445

Day Four: Monday

BREAKFAST   *Calories*

½ small cantaloupe	58
1 slice toast with 1 pat butter	106
1 cup coffee or tea (with/without skim milk and 1 tsp. sugar)......................	0-25

LUNCH

egg salad sandwich with 1 tbsp. mayonnaise and leaf lettuce	310
celery sticks	10
carrot sticks	21
1 small cookie..........................	50
1 cup coffee or tea (with/without skim milk and 1 tsp. sugar), diet soda, water	0-25

DINNER

½ c. spaghetti sauce with meat	125
1 c. spaghetti (4 oz.)	210
lettuce wedge with 1 tbsp. diet dressing ..	40
½ c. zucchini and ½ oz. parmesan cheese..	55
1 glass chianti, diet soda, water	0-100
Total	985-1135

Day Five: Tuesday

BREAKFAST   *Calories*

1 c. unsweetened grapefruit juice	101
1 c. *Special K* cereal (½ c. skim milk and 1 tsp. sugar)............................	129
1 cup coffee or tea (with/without skim milk and 1 tsp. sugar)......................	0-25

LUNCH
McDonald's cheeseburger................. 306
small french fries 211
1 cup coffee or tea (with/without skim milk
    and 1 tsp. sugar), diet soda, water 0-25

DINNER
8 oz. flounder 180
½ c. cole slaw 60
½ c. steamed carrots and 1 pat butter and
    herbs................................ 59
½ cantaloupe 58
1 cup coffee or tea (with/without skim milk
    and 1 tsp. sugar), diet soda, water 0-25

	Total	1104-1179

Day Six: Wednesday

BREAKFAST
Calories

½ papaya 60
1 piece french toast (1 tsp. maple syrup).. 175
1 cup coffee or tea (with/without skim milk
    and 1 tsp. sugar)...................... 0-25

LUNCH
1 c. chicken noodle soup 65
chef salad (lettuce, tomato, 1 slice cheese, 1
    oz. ham, 1 hard-boiled egg, and 1 tbsp.
    diet dressing) 315
1 cup coffee or tea (with/without skim milk
    and 1 tsp. sugar), diet soda, water 0-25

DINNER
½ c. raw spinach salad (1 strip cooked bacon
    and 1 tbsp. diet dressing).............. 91
4 oz. chicken 200
½ c. instant rice 71
½ c. yellow squash steamed with 1 pat
    butter 50
mock melba* 88
1 cup coffee or tea (with/without skim milk
    and 1 tsp. sugar), diet soda, water 0-25

	Total	1115-1190

Day Seven: Thursday

BREAKFAST   Calories
½ grapefruit with ½ tbsp. honey 85
1 c. puffed wheat or puffed cereal (½ c. skim
   milk and 1 tsp. sugar) 110
1 cup coffee or tea (with/without skim milk
   and 1 tsp. sugar) 0-25

LUNCH
⅓ c. cottage cheese with ½ c. fresh fruit on
   lettuce leaf 110
blueberry muffin with 1 pat butter 176
1 cup coffee or tea (with/without skim milk
   and 1 tsp. sugar), diet soda, water 0-25

DINNER
beef kabobs with peppers, tomatoes, and
   mushrooms 260
½ c. mashed potatoes 100
½ c. broccoli steamed with herbs 20
2 small cookies 100
1 cup coffee or tea (with/without skim milk
   and 1 tsp. sugar), diet soda, water 0-25

                Total   961-
                           1036

Chapter 5

Gemini

Gemini, symbolized by twins, rules over third house matters and is guardian of the mind. Gemini is ruled by the agile and quick-witted Mercury. People can always depend on Gemini to say the right thing at the right time. Your responses seem spontaneous. The mind of a Gemini moves at the speed of light. You think more quickly than any of the other signs. Dieting, like almost everything else, is a game to you.

Characteristic of Gemini's twin ruler, you can do two things at the same time and do them equally well. You have the uncanny ability to judge the moods of your companions quite accurately. This, combined with your quick wit, makes you appear truly brilliant to others. Each of your many faces is warm, wonderful, charming and generous. Many believe you are superficial, but this isn't true. You simply have the rare ability to adapt yourself to any situation or environment. This adaptability is true class.

Geminis are not usually emotional. Instead, you tend to analyze everything and everyone. You store away everything you've observed for future reference. Many Geminis have photographic memories. Despite your analytical bent, you believe life is a game, and you play it like a chess master. Mastering all the different moves comes easily to you. The Gemini native is always on his or her toes. You never miss a trick. You learn quickly, and you never forget anything.

Geminis are incurable romantics. People often call you fickle, but that isn't really true. You just crave novelty in your love life. To a Gemini, variety is the spice of life. Once you've mastered all the moves in a relationship, the game becomes less interesting and you want to move on. The only way to hold a Gemini is to let him or her go. But, if a Gemini finds a partner that matches their level of intelligence and energy, they'll stick around to see what happens.

When you're happy, everyone falls in love with you. You can charm even the most critical person. You have a knack for making them feel good about themselves. Geminis like to have a good time. They usually surround themselves with people as imaginative and clever as they are. When you and your friends get together, everyone has a good time.

Geminis are positive people. They can turn the most negative situation into a positive learning experience. The Gemini native sees every person or situation as a challenge that can teach them something of importance about the game of life. Though you Geminis are genuinely interested in other people and what they have to say, you delight in sharing your own knowledge with others. Gemini can best be described as the teacher of the zodiac.

You learn languages easily and write well. You have a talent for expressing yourself and making yourself understood. You can paint instructive and revealing pictures with words.

Geminis are adaptable. They can change to match their surroundings as easily as a chameleon changes colors. Gemini natives enjoy good health. You somehow manage to retain your youthful glow long after your peers have turned to makeup and hair dye. When you do have a problem, it can usually be traced back to nervous tension or stress. Some tension is beneficial, but too much can affect your mental and physical health. Instead of concentrating on one thing at a time, you get excited about all the possibilities, and you can end up causing an accident.

Most Gemini natives do not experience weight problems. You tend to work off your excess fat with that inexhaustible supply of energy. The people who do have problems are usually born in the first or last few days of the sign. If you were born in the closing days of Gemini, you'll find that your weight gain/loss pattern is erratic. Your gains and losses are due, in part, to water retention. Your weight usually follows the path of the moon as it transits through the houses in your horoscope.

Your eating habits cause problems. You are always too busy, so you bolt down your food. What you eat is another common problem for Geminis. You often eat empty calories containing stimulants like caffeine (e.g., coffee, tea, coca cola, chocolate). Try to keep healthier foods at hand for snacks. If you just can't give up the coffee, tea, or chocolate, try cutting back or switching to decaffeinated coffee, herbal tea, or carob, a chocolate substitute.

Geminis sometimes use food as either a tranquilizer or an energizer. If you find you're eating compulsively, stop. Use that Gemini intellect to analyze what you're doing. You may not even realize what or how much you've eaten. You can use the mind-over-matter technique to change your behavior. You'll find it easier to diet if you keep busy doing the things you enjoy. Although you appreciate good food, you appreciate good people much more. You'll find that when you fill your life with other things, food doesn't seem as important as it used to. Wouldn't it be better to eat the kinds of food that are good for you, the kinds that will keep your body in good working order, rather than eat foods that will only sap your strength and leave you feeling poorly? Why not try to become more knowledgeable about what is on the market and what you are putting into your mouth?

Since nicotine and caffeine are stimulants, smoking and

coffee-drinking can make Gemini natives even more nervous. If you smoke, you may find it hard to control the level of tension in your life. That can cause insomnia. With all the energy a Gemini uses during the day, they need a good night's sleep. So learn to smoke and drink coffee in moderation.

Gemini natives don't like competitive sports, so try yoga. You do well in sports that require coordination. You'd probably enjoy golf, gymnastics, or bicycling. Now is the time to get your body back into shape. Because, of all the signs in the zodiac, you retain your youthful looks longer, and, as everybody knows, the first tell-tale sign of age is weight gain.

Don't begin your diet when the sun is in Cancer (June 21-July 20) or Virgo (August 21-September 20). With the many summer social events that include food, you may find yourself giving in to temptation. So enjoy these times with your friends. When the sun enters Libra (September 21-October 20) and when it returns to your birthday, you'll find losing weight easy. Never start your diet before the full moon. Start dieting only after the full moon begins to wane.

Do your grocery shopping for the week on Wednesday. Try to buy more nutritional foods. Every once in a while, treat yourself to something you've really wanted. Then go right back on your diet.

Instead of the usual three meals a day, I've recommended a number of small meals for you Geminis. Eat foods high in fiber content and B-vitamins. These small meals will give you the continuous source of energy you need to keep up your hectic pace.

Suzanne is a typical Gemini—attractive, petite, and energetic. She always manages to keep things exciting. You never know what she'll do next. Suzanne loves to eat, and she exists almost entirely on snacks. She hates to sit down to a leisurely meal, so she usually grabs a bite to eat on her way out. There isn't anything wrong with snacking. It fit Suzanne's lifestyle—the problem was to figure out how she could cut down on junk food, cut calories, and eat more nutritionally.

Suzanne's diet also had to help keep her energy level up and it had to fit her crazy schedule. We hit on something that a doctor had prescribed for little kids, something he called mini-meals, or snacks, and it worked like a charm.

The charts on the following pages will help you find the best time for *you* to lose weight. The easy-to-use astrological wheel has directions on setting up your chart by using your birthday. It shows you how to follow your sun's progress through your twelve houses. The Solar Transit Chart lets you record your weight loss as the sun moves from one house to the next. There is also a first week's menu that will allow you to include the foods you and your family love in your diet.

Familiarize yourself with the astrological wheel and the significance of each house as it pertains to the Gemini native. The houses follow in a counterclockwise circle. Each house covers about a thirty day period.

- When the Gemini sun transits your first house (Gemini), you want to enhance your appearance (weight loss).

- When the Gemini sun transits your second house (Cancer), you want to indulge yourself (weight gain).

- When the Gemini sun transits your third house (Leo), you are better able to express your ideas.

- When the Gemini sun transits your fourth house (Virgo), you want to nurture yourself.

- When the Gemini sun transits your fifth house (Libra), you achieve more confidence in yourself, your appearance, and your abilities (weight loss).

- When the Gemini sun transits your sixth house (Scorpio), you become more interested in your health and working conditions.

- When the Gemini sun transits your seventh house

(Sagittarius), you form new relationships and your interest in other people is renewed.

- When the Gemini sun transits your eighth house (Capricorn), you become more interested in the resources of others as they affect you.

- When the Gemini sun transits your ninth house (Aquarius), you devise new plans for the future.

- When the Gemini sun transits your tenth house (Pisces), you want to move ahead with your career plans.

- When the Gemini sun transits your eleventh house (Aries), you want to cooperate in a group effort.

- When the Gemini sun transits your twelfth house (Taurus), you discover information previously unavailable to you.

- As the sun leaves your twelfth house and prepares to enter your first house again, you will be given a chance to reassess your last solar year and lay plans for the new year ahead.

To personalize the Gemini solar wheel, insert your birthdate in the blank space marked number 1 Gemini. Then, moving counterclockwise, insert the next month and same day in the blank space marked number 2 Cancer. Continue around the solar wheel, marking the month and day in the blank spaces, until you come full circle.

You will now be able to follow the sun's transits through your horoscope and anticipate what aspects of your life will be highlighted each thirty-day period. The transits will also tell you the times during the year you can diet most successfully. For those people born on the cusp of a sign (three days before or three days after) refer to the Solar Position Chart to find out what your sun sign really is.

To see how one dieter personalized his solar wheel, see page 29.

Solar Wheel Chart

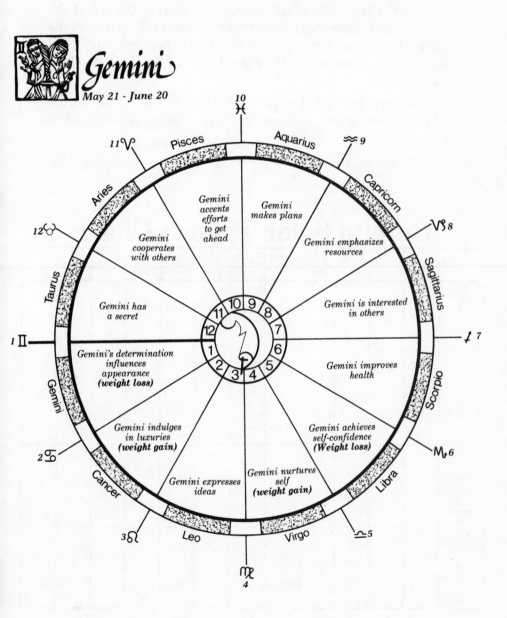

Gemini
May 21 - June 20

10 ♓

11 ♈   Pisces   Aquarius   ♒ 9

Aries   Capricorn

12 ♉   ♑ 8

Gemini makes plans

Gemini accents efforts to get ahead

Gemini cooperates with others

Gemini emphasizes resources

Taurus   Sagittarius

Gemini has a secret

Gemini is interested in others

1 ♊   ♐ 7

Gemini's determination influences appearance *(weight loss)*

Gemini improves health

Gemini

Scorpio

Gemini indulges in luxuries *(weight gain)*

Gemini achieves self-confidence *(Weight loss)*

2 ♋   ♏ 6

Cancer

Gemini expresses ideas

Gemini nurtures self *(weight gain)*

Libra

3 ♌   Leo   Virgo   ♎ 5

♍ 4

The Solar Transit Chart provides you with a guide to those times of the year when you will lose weight and those times you will gain weight.

Insert your birthdate (month and day) at the top of the chart in the space marked number 1 Gemini. Then insert the next month and same day in the space marked number 2 Cancer. Continue across the top of the page until you reach 12 Taurus.

Record your total weight loss or gain with an X. At the end of the solar year, connect the Xs to reveal your astrological pattern.

To see how one dieter recorded her weight, see page 31.

Gemini Solar Transit Chart

House Numbers, Signs and Corresponding Dates

Lbs.	Gemini	Cancer	Leo	Virgo	Libra	Scorpio	Sagittarius	Capricorn	Aquarius	Pisces	Aries	Taurus
10												
9												
8												
7												
6												
5												
4												
3												
2												
1												
–1												
–2												
–3												
–4												
–5												
–6												
–7												
–8												
–9												
–10												

I've outlined a week's worth of menus. Women are allotted 1200 calories, men 1500 calories. Some of the recipes (marked with an asterisk) used in the sample menu can be found in the last chapter of this book. Check the calorie/carbohydrate/protein counter in Appendix C before substituting or exchanging foods.

Gemini: First Week's Menu

Day One: Wednesday

	Calories
BREAKFAST	
1 egg cooked any way	100
1 cup coffee or tea (with/without skim milk and 1 tsp. sugar)......................	0-25
MINI-BREAKFAST	
1 small apple...........................	80
4 oz. orange juice.......................	60
LUNCH	
chef salad (lettuce, tomato, 1 slice cheese, 1 oz. ham, 1 hard cooked egg, and 1 tbsp. diet dressing).........................	315
diet soda, mineral water, water	0-25
MINI-LUNCH	
1 bran muffin and 1 pat butter	136
1 cup coffee or tea (with/without skim milk and 1 tsp. sugar)......................	0-25
DINNER	
stir-fry chicken*	289
½ c. instant rice	71
½ c. steamed carrots and herbs	20
iced herbal tea, mineral water, water	0-25
MINI-DINNER	
1 small fig cookie.......................	50
6 oz. lite cocoa	70
	1191-1291

Day Two: Thursday

	Calories
BREAKFAST	
1 c. puff wheat or puff rice (½ c. skim milk and 1 tsp. sugar)	110
1 cup coffee or tea (with/without skim milk and 1 tsp. sugar)	0-25
SNACK	
Hawaiian breakfast drink	96
LUNCH	
open-face melted cheese sandwich with tomato	185
celery sticks	10
carrot sticks	21
diet soda, mineral water, water	0-25
MINI-LUNCH	
¼ cantaloupe	30
6 oz. apple cider	90
DINNER	
4 oz. lamb chop	140
½ c. broccoli and herbs	20
½ yam baked with 1 pat butter	116
iced herbal tea, mineral water, water	0-25
MINI-DINNER	
¼ c. unshelled pumpkin seeds	60
2 c. lightly salted popcorn	100
6 oz. apple cider	90
Total	1068-1143

Day Three: Friday

	Calories
BREAKFAST	
1 c. oatmeal (with ½ c. skim milk and 1 tsp. sugar)	195
coffee or tea (with/without skim milk and 1 tsp. sugar)	0-25

MINI-BREAKFAST

1 orange	65
1 piece of whole wheat toast with 1 pat butter	101
4 oz. skim milk.........................	45

LUNCH

2 tacos................................	360
diet soda, mineral water, water	0-25

MINI-LUNCH

½ c. yogurt with ½ c. strawberries........	65
herbal tea..............................	0

DINNER

vegetable omelette*.....................	260
lettuce and tomato salad with 1 tbsp. diet dressing	60
iced herbal tea, mineral water, water	0-25

MINI-DINNER

1 c. chicken bouillon....................	20
2 saltine crackers	25
Total	**1196-1271**

Day Four: Saturday

BREAKFAST

	Calories
½ small cantaloupe	60
1 cup coffee or tea (with/without skim milk and 1 tsp. sugar)	0-25

MINI-BREAKFAST

4 oz. orange juice......................	60
corn muffin and 1 pat butter	166

LUNCH

4 oz. shrimp salad	210
1 c. chicken with rice soup..............	45
diet soda, mineral water, water	0-25

MINI-LUNCH

stuffed celery*	40
4 oz. vegetable juice	20

DINNER

lamb curry	290
½ c. noodles	100
lettuce and tomato salad with 1 tbsp. diet dressing	60
iced herbal tea, mineral water, water	0-25

MINI-DINNER

½ apple	35
1 oz. swiss cheese	105
1 cup herbal tea	0-25
Total	1191-1291

Day Five: Sunday

BREAKFAST

	Calories
6 oz. grapefruit juice	75
1 piece french toast (1 tsp. maple syrup)	175
1 cup coffee or tea (with/without skim milk and 1 tsp. sugar)	0-25

MINI-BREAKFAST

½ c. fresh strawberries	20
8 oz. skim milk	90

LUNCH

½ c. plain cottage cheese with tomato on lettuce leaf	130
1 hard cooked egg	82
diet soda, mineral water, water	0-25

MINI-LUNCH

1 oz. cheese and 4 saltine crackers	160
1 glass dry wine	85

DINNER

4 oz. broiled fillet of sole	80
4 stalks asparagus with herb or lemon juice	10
spaghetti squash with 1 pat butter	100

iced herbal tea, mineral water,
    water 0-25

MINI-DINNER
baked apple............................ 130
herbal tea............................. 0-25
                                 _____
                          Total 1137-
                                 1237

Day Six: Monday

BREAKFAST   Calories
1 blueberry muffin with 1 pat
    butter 176
coffee or tea (with/without skim
    milk and 1 tsp. sugar)................ 0-25

MINI-BREAKFAST
4 oz. orange juice...................... 60
fruit salad 126

LUNCH
3½ oz. shrimp with cocktail sauce 125
½ c. Manhattan clam chowder 35
diet soda, mineral water, water 0-25

MINI-LUNCH
celery sticks 10
carrot sticks 21
radishes 5
dip 30
4 oz. vegetable juice 20

DINNER
4 oz. steak 235
½ baked potato with 1 pat butter or 1
    tbsp. sour cream and chives 111
lettuce and tomato salad with
    1 tbsp. diet dressing 60
iced herbal tea, mineral water,
    water 0-25

MINI-DINNER
strawberry shortcake................... 140

decaffeinated coffee or herbal tea
(with/without skim milk and
1 tsp. sugar)   0-25

Total   1154-
1254

Day Seven: Tuesday

BREAKFAST Calories
½ freshly squeezed lemon in 1 cup
hot water with 1 tsp. honey   35
1 piece whole wheat toast with 1
pat butter   101
1 cup coffee or tea (with/without
skim milk and 1 tsp. sugar)   0-25

MINI-BREAKFAST
5 dried apricots or 3 fresh
apricots   55
4 oz. skim milk   45

LUNCH
McDonald's cheeseburger   306
diet soda, mineral water, water   0-25

MINI-LUNCH
zucchini and cucumber chips   20
cherry tomatoes   20
herbal tea   0-25

DINNER
½ 10″ cheese pizza   500
salad and 1 tbsp. diet dressing   60
iced herbal tea, mineral water,
water   0-25

MINI-DINNER
yogurt shake*, pineapple   135

Total   1277-
1377

Chapter 6

Cancer

Cancer, the moon child, is ruled by the moon. Unlike most of the other signs, your weight increases or decreases depending on the phase of the moon. Most Cancers can gain or lose five to ten pounds in one month without changing their eating or drinking habits.

Cancer is the first of the water signs and the second cardinal sign in the zodiac. Your symbol, the self-protecting crab, rules over the fourth house: home, family, caring, and sharing. Cancers like nothing better than mothering and protecting people. You may become depressed if you aren't nurturing someone. No problem is too big, no worry too small for your notice.

Not only are you generous, you're also easygoing. You tend to approach situations in a slow and indirect way. This characteristic may lead people to believe you are weak and indecisive. It isn't true. What most people don't realize is: what Cancer wants, Cancer eventually gets. You have the patience to wait for what you want. You never approach your goals directly. You keep your own counsel, and while others are talking or fighting about what they want, you quietly move in and take the prize, much to the surprise of everyone around you. Never underestimate a Cancer.

As a water sign, you live by the motto, "I feel." You rely more on your intuition than on your intellect, and you're rarely wrong. You never miss a trick. Cancer has the best and most accurate memory of any of the signs.

Although you love to be part of a group you're basically an introvert. As a cardinal sign and, therefore, good at keeping secrets, you prefer to work alone. You need the freedom to take the initiative and act independently. Like Gemini, there are two sides to your personality. People see you as tough, but deep down where their glances don't penetrate, you're a creative, sensitive, sympathetic person. Your heart is always in the right place.

Cancers are lucky gamblers because they only bet on a sure thing. It may not seem like a sure thing to anyone else, but you've sized up the situation before taking action. After assessing the facts, you use your uncanny intuition to come to a conclusion (and you're usually right).

Violence is hard for you to understand, and you'll go to great lengths to avoid a confrontation. But, God help anyone who threatens your home or family. You'll fight to the death to protect the people you love. You have a knack for knowing where your opponent is vulnerable.

You relate especially well to children. Children know instinctively you're a person they can trust. You have a great deal of love to give, but because of your generous nature, you, of all the signs of the zodiac, are probably the easiest to take advantage of. Cancers are true romantics, and not just about children.

The primary concern of any Cancer native is a home they can call their own. Your security is being surrounded by familiar objects and beloved people. You're at your best in this kind of environment. Being invited into the home of a Cancer native is always a pleasure. You can put people at ease and make them feel right at home. Everyone usually gravitates to a Cancer's kitchen, for it's a wonderful hodgepodge of sights, sounds, and smells. There are always chocolate chip cookies in the oven; the latest in kitchen appliances on the counter, the pictures the kids have done hanging on the refrigerator, an old Valentine's Day card pinned to the bulletin board, and the smell of fresh coffee brewing. The first thing the Cancer host or hostess will do is make their guest sit down at a big, old-fashioned antique table that has been in the family for years and offer them a cup of coffee and something to eat.

Cancers love to eat, and most Cancers are fabulous cooks. But you can be your own worst enemy when it comes to food. You often turn to food when you are upset, feel in need of love, or feel your hard-won sense of your security is slipping.

Water retention is your worst problem. Your weight fluctuates wildly—from a few pounds to a dress size. You're the person who can diet religiously and suddenly gain five pounds overnight. No one will believe you didn't cheat. Many Cancers have two wardrobes, and they sometimes use both in the same month. You'll probably lose and gain more weight in a lifetime than all the other signs in the zodiac put together.

Cancers are represented by water in its liquid state, and are strong-willed and persistent. Your will is like the tide wearing away the rocky shore, ultimately, the shore must conform to the water's power. But, like the water you represent, you often follow the path of least resistance. In the case of dieting, any emotional upheaval sends you back to the comfort of food. You'll have to learn how to reach for a different kind of comfort. Since the kitchen is your favorite place to be, why not experiment with cutting calories in your favorite recipes or try the new *cuisine minceur* (low-calorie cooking)?

You love food and your home cooking has probably won raves from your family and neighbors if not from the media and awards at County Fairs and bake-offs. You not only love to prepare it, but you do enjoy eating it as well.

Most overweight Cancers are compulsive eaters. When you find yourself overeating, try not to overload your system with heavy, greasy foods. Since fats are the hardest substance to digest, this could cause problems ranging from a mild upset stomach to an ulcer. If at all possible, avoid binging when you're upset. Instead of food, reach for someone you love and talk out your problem. You do so much for others, let them help you once in a while.

Cancers usually have three reasons for overeating: (1) you overeat when you feel threatened or insecure; (2) you overeat in times of great stress; (3) you sometimes get a terrible craving for sweets. In some unusual cases, Cancers have been known to use fat as a comfortable shell to protect them against real or imaginary hurts. Giving up the image of yourself as fat and letting the world see the skinny, beautiful you can be difficult.

When you've started to plan your diet, begin by cutting your salt intake by half, if not more. This will alleviate your water retention problem. Next, cut down on refined sugars, flour, and fats. Substitute natural sweeteners and add more fiber to your diet.

Begin to record your weight daily. Weigh yourself first thing in the morning without clothes. This should give you an accurate reading. You'll find your weight loss has a definite pattern. You, more than any of the other signs, are affected by the phases of the moon. You'll probably discover that you gain weight more readily just before or just after a full moon.

If you begin your diet when your sun is in Cancer (June 21-July 20) or Scorpio (October 21-November 20), it can be easy and fun. The pounds will seem to melt away. Be sure to start your diet on the first Monday after the full moon. That way you won't retain as much fluid. The first day of your diet consists only of liquids supplemented with a high-potency vitamin tablet. This should shrink your stomach and flush out your system. Remain on this diet for *one day* only, no longer. Check with your doctor before starting this or any other diet.

After the twenty-four hours on your liquid diet, begin eating the lighter meals outlined in your first week's menu (1200 calories for women to 1500 calories for men). Eat more of the fresh fruits and vegetables, drink fruit juices, and enjoy fish, especially shellfish, and poultry. Use salt, oils, and fats sparingly.

If you start dieting when the sun is in your second house, Leo (July 21-August 20), or your fourth house, Libra (September 21-October 20), don't be discouraged if you can't seem to lose weight. These are the worst possible times for you to begin a diet. It's not that you can't diet, but you may get easily discouraged by the lack of results.

With the new findings about the dangers of additives, refined sugar and flour, you should think seriously about making your own bread. Since Cancers have green thumbs, you might want to grow your own fruits and vegetables.

Or take up fishing, crabbing, or clamming. They're all relaxing hobbies that give you either time to yourself or an enjoyable outdoor activity to share with your children. The fresh air, good exercise, and the possibility of a fresh seafood dinner are added bonuses. Seafood can do wonders for your figure, complexion, and digestive tract.

You aren't known for your strength, stamina, or agility, but since you love water, swimming, snorkeling, or scuba diving are naturals for you. You don't enjoy competition, and, consequently, rigorous sports aren't for you. You may dislike competition because it can lower not only your self-esteem, but your opponent's self-esteem if he loses, so it may be better not to get involved with competitive sports.

A diet group like Weight Watchers or Diet Center may be just the thing for you. Cancers are supportive of others and receptive to encouragement from others. Nothing will make you stray from your diet faster than depression or a bout with low self-esteem. Bur remember, a beautiful, healthy body is the perfect cure for poor self-image.

Jodi is your typical moon child. She has a lovely, round face, a round body, and a Cancer's love of desserts. Cooking is one of her hobbies, and you can see she enjoys the fruits of her labors. Before she went back to work as an agricultural engineer and a garden columnist for a local paper she used to bake all her own bread, make cakes and cookies from scratch, and grow many of her own fruits and vegetables. With the pressures of home, family, and work, Jodi gained a considerable amount of weight.

She started her diet right after the full moon as part of her birthday celebration. She really lost weight, but she seemed to hit a plateau in her second month. All the temporary lull meant was that her body was adjusting to the tremendous weight loss. It gave her a chance to catch up. After the full moon waned again, her weight loss continued, and she treated herself to a new bathing suit and a trip to the beach.

The charts on the following pages will help you find the best time for *you* to lose weight. The easy-to-use astrological wheel has directions on setting up your chart by using your birthday. It shows you how to follow your sun's progress through your twelve houses. The Solar Transit Chart lets you record your weight loss as the sun moves from one house to the next. There is also a first week's menu that will allow you to include the foods you and your family love in your diet.

Familiarize yourself with the astrological wheel and the significance of each house as it pertains to the Cancer native. The houses follow in a counterclockwise circle. Each house covers about a thirty-day period.

- When the Cancer sun transits your first house (Cancer), you want to enhance your appearance (weight loss).

- When the Cancer sun transits your second house (Leo), you want to indulge yourself (weight gain).

- When the Cancer sun transits your third house (Virgo), you are better able to express your ideas.

- When the Cancer sun transits your fourth house (Libra), you want to nurture yourself.

- When the Cancer sun transits your fifth house (Scorpio), you achieve more confidence in yourself, your appearance, and your abilities (weight loss).

- When the Cancer sun transits your sixth house (Sagittarius), you become more interested in your health and working conditions.

- When the Cancer sun transits your seventh house (Capricorn), you form new relationships and your interest in other people is renewed.

- When the Cancer sun transits your eighth house (Aquarius), you become more interested in the resources of others as they affect you.

- When the Cancer sun transits your ninth house (Pisces), you devise new plans for the future.

- When the Cancer sun transits your tenth house (Aries), you want to move ahead with your career plans.

- When the Cancer sun transits your eleventh house (Taurus), you want to cooperate in a group effort.

- When the Cancer sun transits your twelfth house (Gemini), you discover information previously unavailable to you.

- As the sun leaves your twelfth house and prepares to enter your first house again, you will be given a chance to reassess your last solar year and lay plans for the new year ahead.

To personalize your solar wheel, insert your birthdate in the blank space marked number 1 Cancer. Then, moving counterclockwise, insert the next month and same day in the blank space marked number 2 Leo. Continue around the solar wheel, marking the month and day in the blank spaces, until you come full circle.

You will now be able to follow the sun's transits through your horoscope and anticipate what areas of your life will be highlighted each thirty-day period. The transits will also tell you the times during the year dieting will be most successful. For those people who are born on the cusp of a sign (three days before or three days after) refer to the Solar Position Chart to find out what your sun sign really is.

To see how one dieter personalized his solar wheel, see page 29.

Solar Wheel Chart

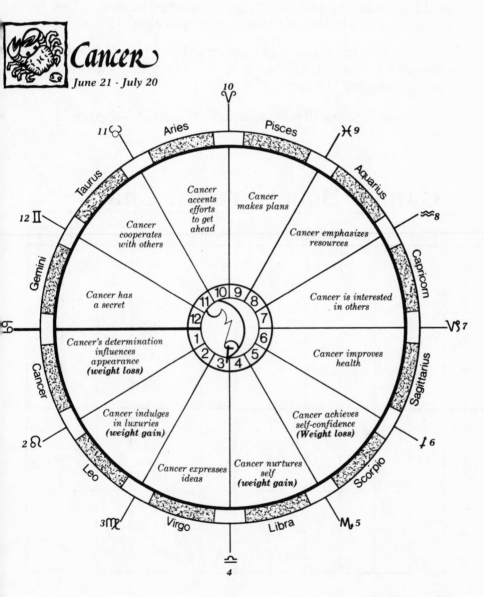

Cancer

June 21 - July 20

Cancer accents efforts to get ahead

Cancer makes plans

Cancer cooperates with others

Cancer emphasizes resources

Cancer has a secret

Cancer is interested in others

Cancer's determination influences appearance *(weight loss)*

Cancer improves health

Cancer indulges in luxuries *(weight gain)*

Cancer achieves self-confidence *(Weight loss)*

Cancer expresses ideas

Cancer nurtures self *(weight gain)*

The Solar Transit Chart provides you with a guide to those times of the year when you will lose weight and those times you will gain weight.

Insert your birthdate (month and day) at the top of the chart in the space marked number 1 Cancer. Then insert the next month and same day in the space marked number 2 Leo. Continue across the top of the page until you reach 12 Gemini.

Record your total weight loss or gain with an X (see the example). At the end of the solar year, connect the Xs to reveal your astrological pattern.

To see how one dieter recorded her weight, see page 31.

Cancer Solar Transit Chart

	House Numbers, Signs and Corresponding Dates											
Lbs.	Cancer	Leo	Virgo	Libra	Scorpio	Sagittarius	Capricorn	Aquarius	Pisces	Aries	Taurus	Gemini
10												
9												
8												
7												
6												
5												
4												
3												
2												
1												
−1												
−2												
−3												
−4												
−5												
−6												
−7												
−8												
−9												
−10												

Use the following week's menus (1200 calories for women, 1500 calories for men) as a planning guide. Some of the recipes (marked with an asterisk) used in this chapter can be found in Chapter 15. Check substitutions and exchanges in the calorie/carbohydrate/protein counter in Appendix C.

Cancer: First Week's Menu

Day One: Monday

BREAKFAST
vegetable juice (any kind)
8 oz. milk
1 cup coffee or tea (with/without skim milk
    and 1 tsp. sugar)
water

LUNCH
chicken bouillon
1 cup coffee or tea (with/without skim milk
    and 1 tsp. sugar)
diet soda, water

DINNER
fruit soup
vegetable juice (any kind)
jello made with fruit juice and 1 tbsp. cream
    topping
1 cup coffee or tea (with/without skim milk
    and 1 tsp. sugar), diet soda, water

Use this menu on the first day of your diet only. Any amount of juice, soup, or other liquids you like can be substituted for those in the first day's menu.

Day Two: Tuesday

BREAKFAST Calories

½ c. oatmeal (with ½ c. skim milk plus
    1 tsp. sugar) 104
8 oz. orange juice........................ 120
1 cup coffee or tea (with/without skim milk
    and 1 tsp. sugar) 0-25

LUNCH

1 c. clam chowder 100
lettuce and tomato salad (1 tbsp. diet
    dressing) 60
1 apple and 1 oz. cheese 180
iced tea, coffee, diet soda, water.......... 0-25

DINNER

shrimp with almonds* 245
½ c. instant rice 90
broccoli with cheese* 160
¼ cantaloupe cut into chunks and ½ c. fresh
    strawberries over 2 oz. vanilla
ice cream 125
1 cup coffee or tea (with/without skim milk
    and 1 tsp. sugar), diet soda, water 0-25

Total   1184-
1259

Day Three: Wednesday

BREAKFAST Calories

6 oz. cranberry juice 123
1 egg cooked any way 100
1 slice of toast with 1 pat butter.......... 100
1 cup coffee or tea (with/without skim milk
    and 1 tsp. sugar)...................... 0-25

LUNCH

½ c. tuna salad with fruit or vegetables... 200
2 saltines 25
iced tea, coffee, diet soda, water.......... 0-25

DINNER

1 c. macaroni and cheese	430
½ c. fresh steamed broccoli with 1 pat butter	55
lettuce wedge and 1 tbsp. diet dressing ...	30
coffee or tea (with/without skim milk and 1 tsp. sugar), diet soda, water	0-25
Total	1038-1113

Day Four: Thursday

BREAKFAST <small>Calories</small>

½ cantaloupe	40
yogurt shake	135
coffee or tea (with/without skim milk and 1 tsp. sugar)	0-25

LUNCH

open turkey sandwich	185
1 tbsp. cranberry sauce.................	25
lettuce and tomato salad (1 tbsp. diet dressing)	60
iced tea, coffee, diet soda, water..........	0-25
dessert of your choice..................	200

DINNER

New England style fish.................	180
1 baked potato with 1 pat butter	110
mixed fresh vegetables (steamed)	45
1 fried banana and 1 tbsp. whipped cream	145
coffee or tea (with/without skim milk and 1 tsp. sugar), diet soda, water	0-25
Total	1125-1200

Day Five: Friday

BREAKFAST <small>Calories</small>

cheese sandwich on 1 slice whole wheat bread	165
2 strips bacon	85

coffee or tea (with/without skim milk and
1 tsp. sugar) 0-25

LUNCH
McDonald's cheeseburger 306
small french fries 211
iced tea, coffee, diet soda, water 0-25

DINNER
4 oz. spiced shrimp 108
½ c. rice pilaf 90
½ c. raw spinach salad and 1 strip crumbled
bacon (1 tbsp. diet dressing) 91
1 small cheesecake* 170
coffee or tea (with/without skim milk and
1 tsp. sugar), diet soda, water 0-25

Total   1226-
1301

Day Six: Saturday

BREAKFAST   Calories
½ grapefruit and 1 tbsp. honey 110
1 bran muffin and 1 pat butter 140
coffee or tea (with/without skim milk and
1 tsp. sugar) 0-25

LUNCH
1 c. crab salad on endive lettuce 155
1 c. vegetable beef soup 80
2 saltine crackers 25
3 oz. ice cream 100
iced tea, coffee, diet soda, water 0-25

DINNER
veal cutlet 185
½ baked potato with 1 pat butter or 1 tbsp.
sour cream and chives 110
½ c. steamed winter squash with Italian
spices 65
1 glass rose wine 65
coffee or tea (with/without skim milk and
1 tsp. sugar), diet soda, water 0-25

Total   1055-
1130

Day Seven: Sunday

BREAKFAST Calories

1 poached egg...........................	100
1 slice toast with 1 pat butter............	100
6 oz. apple juice........................	120
coffee or tea (with/without skim milk and 1 tsp. sugar).........................	0-25

LUNCH

fruit salad on lettuce leaf...............	126
½ c. cottage cheese (mixed with raisins and dates)....................	200
1 blueberry muffin plus 1 pat butter.....	145
iced tea, coffee, diet soda, water..........	0-25

DINNER

1 lb. lobster with 1 tsp. butter...........	212
½ c. fresh steamed asparagus with almonds.......................	40
mixed green salad and 1 tbsp. diet dressing.............................	60
1 glass white wine....................	85
coffee or tea (with/without skim milk and 1 tsp. sugar), diet soda, water.........	0-25
Total	1226-1301

Chapter 7

Leo

All the known planets in our solar system revolve around the sun. The sun makes life on Earth possible. Leo's symbol of power is the lion, king of beasts, your ruler is the sun. Leo is characterized by romance, love of children, creativity, risk-taking, the ability to enjoy life. There is never a dull moment in the life of a Leo.

Leo rules in the fifth house. Natives of this sign are sure of who they are, what they want, and where they want to go. Leos thrive in a position of authority where you can do the most good for the greatest number of people, of course. But, you need not worry, you will be able to obtain a position of power no matter what endeavor you decide on because you are a natural born leader.

You never abuse your authority. You'd never dream of hurting someone, and you can't believe anyone else would. The hardest lesson for a Leo to learn is that not everyone is as nice as they are. Even when people let you down, it's hard for you to hold a grudge. If they apologize, you're more than willing to forgive and forget. You have a reputation as a soft touch.

You take your responsibilities seriously. That's one of the reasons you're well-liked. As a Leo native, you have a panache and self-confidence that inspires others. You know instinctively what needs to be done in any given situation. You always forge ahead, issuing orders and getting the job done.

There's nothing petty about Leos. For them, happiness is making others happy. The Leo native needs more love and understanding than any of the other signs in the zodiac. The approval of others is important, and you'll do anything, short of being mean, to win it.

You enjoy life, work hard, play hard, and, above all, you love gently. There is no lover more tender, more thoughtful than a Leo. You are an incurable romantic. You may like to surprise your lover with a candlelit dinner with all the trimmings. Or, if it's a beautiful day, a picnic lunch, complete with wine, bread, cheese, grapes, and a kite for the kids.

You have a gift for making other people happy. If a Leo can't pry a smile or coax a laugh from someone, nobody can. Many great entertainers are Leos. If you're a Leo, you either are or have wanted to be connected with the entertainment business. But if you don't make it in show business, you could always run for president.

You love children, but unlike the Cancer who wants to protect them, Leos want to play with them. You're the parent every child wishes they had. You're a kindred spirit. You're a lot like a child yourself. Having Leo for a parent would be like having Lucille Ball and Robert Redford as parents. Now, wouldn't any child love that!

You have a strong personality. You're ambitious, but rarely at the expense of others. You have the ability to bring out the best in people. People automatically feel comfortable with you, while at the same time being impressed with your abilities. It's easy for you to get people to see things your way. Since Leo is a fixed fire sign, you may not realize how much power you wield and how many people you influence. Leo is the most powerful, positive sign in the zodiac. You have foresight, determination, and courage. You're a positive thinker, and this, combined with your true grit, ensures you will accomplish whatever you set your mind to do.

Like their symbol, the lion, Leos usually have beautiful, well-groomed hair. You can dress to create an illusion of mystery, glamour, or a drama. It all depends on what you want people to see. Because you do like to look your best, you're usually in good health. Dieting is not much of a problem for Leos. Leos tend to gain weight as they get older—the pounds sneak up on you. It didn't happen overnight, it was one pound at a time, one to two pounds a year and in ten years you are looking at 20 extra pounds—and you know what that means. By middle age you have what is known as "middle age spread." You probably gained so gradually that you didn't notice anything unusual until someone said, "You've gained a few pounds since I saw you." Nothing mortifies a Leo more than feeling they don't look their best. The worst part of this kind of weight is that it all settles right there in the middle. This is the worst fat of all because it is the worst fat in the world to get rid of and you don't even remember gaining it and it's been there a long time. Losing your weight requires dieting and exercise. When you lose (and you will) the skin may have strengthened over the years to accommodate your weight gain. If you do not incorporate exercise to encourage it to return to its natural state, then you may find that you have stretch marks.

Bonnie, a typical untypical Leo, is the owner of one of Washington, D.C.'s up-and-coming graphic design studios. Like most Leos, she is beautiful, talented, and creative.

We happened to meet over lunch at a fashionable Mexican restaurant (where else would you expect to find a Leo?). When we were discussing *Diet Signs*, Bonnie revealed that she'd always had a weight problem. She used to tip the scales at 147 pounds. I couldn't believe this gorgeous creature knew the meaning of the word overweight. Three years ago on December 1, when the sun entered her fifth house, Bonnie went on a diet and lost seven pounds the first week and ten more pounds in the next three weeks as the sun crossed her fifth house. She's kept it off ever since. I asked her if there was a secret to her success. She winked and said, "Champagne has always helped me lose weight."

When it comes to good food and wine, Leos know the difference between domestic and French champagnes. It's only the best for you and your guests. You are the best host or hostess in the zodiac. You're the kind of cook that can step into the kitchen and whip up a little elegant something in a few minutes. Your meals are works of art that make the guests applaud. You love being appreciated, and you'll invite everyone back for an encore.

Leo likes nothing better than a party, but beware. If your socializing is centered around food—inviting people in for brunch, meeting the boys or girls for lunch, stopping for tea after shopping, cocktails before dinner, dinner, dessert and coffee after the theater—it can wreak havoc with your diet. From now on, take note of the nutritional value and the carbo-hydrate/calorie/protein count of what you eat.

Since you take such pride in your appearance, a glance at your reflection in a full-length mirror is quite an incentive to stick to your diet. A mirror doesn't lie.

The Sunday after the full moon is the best day to begin your diet. If you begin your diet before the full moon, you won't see dramatic results. Your best times during the year to begin a diet are when the sun enters Leo (July 21-August 20), and again when it enters Sagittarius (November 21-December 20). The sun is at its most powerful during these times, and that will help you lose. If you delay your diet until the sun enters Virgo (August 21-September 20) or Scorpio (October 21-November 20) you may see little weight loss, and that can be discouraging.

Leo rules the heart, so don't put undue stress on your heart. Cut down on your intake of salt and polyunsaturated fats. If you smoke, it would be wise to give up cigarettes or cigars. Give up or cut down on the amount of coffee you drink.

This advice may be good for your health, but bad for your diet, since you'll be tempted to use food as a stopgap.

Once you've made up your mind to diet, you won't have any trouble losing weight. Fire signs burn off calories rapidly when they're young, but as you get older, you may be less active, neglect your diet, or fail to exercise regularly. So learn more about nutrition now before it's too late to get back into shape. Adopt good eating and exercise habits now. Try organizing a baseball team or a soccer team. When the baseball season is over, take up tennis or jogging. Since Leos tend to jump right into things, begin exercising gradually. Don't overdo the first time on the court. You could strain your muscles or hurt your back.

If you hate exercising, think about trying out for a local theater group. Leos make wonderful actors, being on center stage will provide you with an added incentive to lose weight. Who knows, it might even lead to a professional acting job— anything is possible for a Leo.

The charts on the following pages will help you find the best time for *you* to lose weight. The easy-to-use astrological wheel has directions on setting up your chart by using your birthday. It shows you how to follow your sun's progress through your twelve houses. The Solar Transit Chart lets you record your weight loss as the sun moves from one house to the next. There is also a first week's menu that will allow you to include the foods you and your family love in your diet.

Familiarize yourself with the astrological wheel and the significance of each house as it pertains to the Leo native. The houses follow in a counterclockwise circle. Each house covers about a thirty-day period.

- When the Leo sun transits your first house (Leo), you want to enhance your appearance (weight loss).

- When the Leo sun transits your second house (Virgo), you want to indulge yourself (weight gain).

- When the Leo sun transits your third house (Libra), you are better able to express your ideas.

- When the Leo sun transits your fourth house (Scorpio), you want to nurture yourself.

- When the Leo sun transits your fifth house (Sagittarius), you achieve more confidence in yourself, your appearance, and your abilities (weight loss).

- When the Leo sun transits your sixth house (Capricorn), you become more interested in your health and working conditions.

- When the Leo sun transits your seventh house (Aquarius), you form new relationships and your interest in other people is renewed.

- When the Leo sun transits your eighth house (Pisces), you become more interested in the resources of others as they affect you.

- When the Leo sun transits your ninth house (Aries), you devise new plans for the future.

- When the Leo sun transits your tenth house (Taurus), you want to move ahead with your career plans.

- When the Leo sun transits your eleventh house (Gemini), you want to cooperate in a group effort.

- When the Leo sun transits your twelfth house (Cancer), you discover information previously unavailable to you.

- As the sun leaves your twelfth house and prepares to enter your first house again, you will be given a chance to reassess your last solar year and lay plans for the new year ahead.

To personalize your solar wheel, insert your birthdate (month and day) in the blank space marked number 1 Leo. Then, moving counterclockwise, insert the next month and same day in the blank space marked number 2 Virgo. Continue around the solar wheel marking the month and day in the blank spaces until you come full circle.

You will now be able to follow the sun's transits through your horoscope and anticipate what areas of your life will be highlighted each thirty-day period. The transits will also tell you the times during the year dieting will be most successful. For those people who are born on the cusp of a sign (three days before or three days after), refer to the Solar Position Chart to find out what your sun really is.

To see how one dieter personalized his solar wheel, see page 29.

Solar Wheel Chart

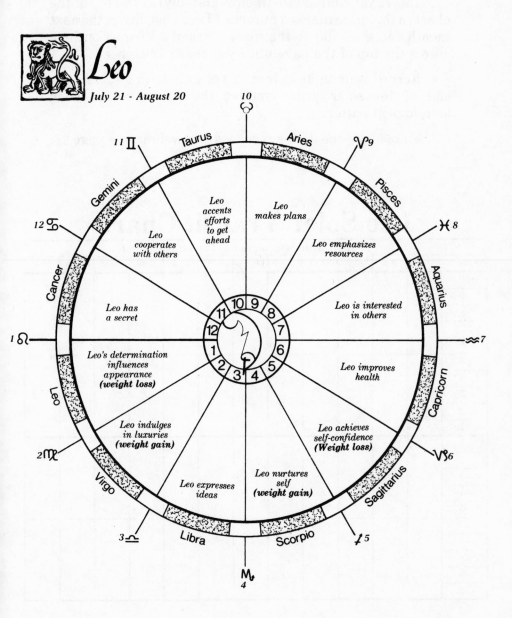

Leo

July 21 - August 20

10

11 Ⅱ — Taurus — Aries — ♈9

Gemini — Pisces

12 ♋ — Leo accents efforts to get ahead — Leo makes plans — ♓ 8

Leo cooperates with others — Leo emphasizes resources

Cancer — Aquarius

Leo has a secret — Leo is interested in others

11 10 9
12 — 8
— 7
1 — 6
2 3 4 5

1 ♌ — ≈ 7

Leo's determination influences appearance **(weight loss)** — Leo improves health

Leo

Leo indulges in luxuries **(weight gain)** — Leo achieves self-confidence **(Weight loss)**

2 ♍ — ♑ 6

Virgo — Sagittarius

Leo expresses ideas — Leo nurtures self **(weight gain)**

3 ♎ — Libra — Scorpio — ♐ 5

♏ 4

The Solar Transit Chart provides you with a guide to those times of the year when you will lose weight and those times you will gain weight.

Insert your birthdate (month and day) at the top of the chart in the space marked number 1 Leo. Then insert the next month and same day in the space marked 2 Virgo. Continue across the top of the page until you reach 12 Cancer.

Record your total weight loss or gain with an X. At the end of the solar year, connect the Xs to reveal your astrological pattern.

To see how one dieter recorded her weight, see page 31.

Leo Solar Transit Chart

House Numbers, Signs and Corresponding Dates

Lbs.	Leo	Virgo	Libra	Scorpio	Sagittarius	Capricorn	Aquarius	Pisces	Aries	Taurus	Gemini	Cancer
10												
9												
8												
7												
6												
5												
4												
3												
2												
1												
-1												
-2												
-3												
-4												
-5												
-6												
-7												
-8												
-9												
-10												

There are many diets to choose from. You fuel-efficient Leos should consider a low carbohydrate diet. Use meats, poultry, fish, and fresh fruits and vegetables. Drink plenty of water—at least eight glasses a day. Never start this or any other diet without consulting your doctor.

The following diet plan allows you sixty grams of carbohydrates per day. Check the calorie/carbohydrate/protein counter in Appendix C before substituting or exchanging food. Recipes for some of the suggested dishes (marked with an asterisk) appear in Chapter 15.

Leo: First Week's Menu

Day One: Sunday

BRUNCH   Carbohydrates (in grams)

8 oz. V-8 juice......................... 9
2 chicken in the basket 18
Canadian bacon (unlimited amount)...... 0
hot lemonade*.......................... 8

DINNER

turkey au jus (unlimited amount) 1
½ c. mashed potatoes 14
asparagus (with butter or hollandaise
    sauce) 4
fresh strawberries in champagne 8
1 glass dry white wine (chablis, rhine).... 1
coffee or tea (with/without heavy cream) . 0-1

Total   63-64

Day Two: Monday

BREAKFAST   Carbohydrates (in grams)

1 c. Kellogg's *Special K* cereal with ¼ c.
    light cream, and 1 tsp. sugar 5
coffee or tea (with/without heavy cream) . 0-1

LUNCH

beef noodle soup........................	5
chicken salad	2
iced tea, coffee, diet soda, water..........	0-1

DINNER

Florida cocktail*	18
chili	9
piece of cheddar cheese.................	1
avocado, lettuce and tomato salad (go light on dressing)	5
martini or scotch on the rocks before dinner................................	1
coffee or tea (with/without heavy cream) .	0-1
Total	**53-56**

Day Three: Tuesday

BREAKFAST Carbohydrates (in grams)

eggs fried in butter (unlimited amount) ..	1
1 slice of protein toast with butter........	9
8 oz. V-8 juice..........................	9
coffee or tea (with/without heavy cream) .	0-1

LUNCH

hamburger patty (unlimited amount) with cheese	1
lettuce and tomato salad (use dressing sparingly)	6
iced tea, coffee, diet soda, water..........	0-1

DINNER

Hawaiian chicken*	11
½ c. rice	21
1 glass dry white wine (chablis, rhine)....	1
coffee or tea (with/without heavy cream) .	0-1
Total	**59-62**

Day Four: Wednesday

BREAKFAST   Carbohydrates (in grams)

plain yogurt with fresh unsweetened fruit
    and 1 tbsp. wheat germ
coffee or tea (with/without heavy cream) .   0-1

LUNCH

chicken bouillon   0
chef salad (use dressing sparingly)   6
iced tea, coffee, diet soda, water..........   0-1

DINNER

pork chops (unlimited amount)...........   0
potato salad   12
green beans in butter with slivered
    almonds   6
1 glass dry red wine (claret, burgundy) ..   1
coffee or tea (with/without heavy cream) .   0-1

                           Total   54-57

Day Five: Thursday

BREAKFAST   Carbohydrates (in grams)

6 oz. orange juice.......................   8
hard-boiled eggs (unlimited)   1
piece of cheddar or hard cheese   1
coffee or tea (with/without heavy cream) .   0-1

LUNCH

tuna salad   3
cherry tomatoes   4
4 Ritz crackers........................   8
iced tea, coffee, diet soda, water..........   0-1

DINNER

pot roast with potatoes, celery, carrots,
    and onions..........................   21
salad with lettuce, tomato, grated cheddar
    cheese   6
1 glass dry red wine (claret, burgundy) ..   1
coffee or tea (with/without heavy cream) .   0-1

                           Total   53-56

Day Six: Friday

BREAKFAST   Carbohydrates (in grams)

8 oz. V-8 juice........................... 9
1 bran muffin with butter and/or cream
    cheese................................ 15
coffee or tea (with/without heavy cream) . 0-1

LUNCH

2 tacos or an egg salad sandwich on
    protein bread........................ 18
carrot sticks 5
iced tea, coffee, diet soda, water.......... 0-1

DINNER

fish cooked in butter (unlimited) 0
broccoli with cheese sauce 5
lettuce wedge sprinkled with grated
    cheese and chopped hard-boiled egg
    (roquefort or oil and vinegar
    dressing) 4
1 glass dry white wine (chablis, rhine).... 1
coffee or tea (with/without heavy cream) . 0-1

                      Total 57-60

Day Seven: Saturday

BRUNCH   Carbohydrates (in grams)

1 c. cottage cheese...................... 5
ambrosia* 21
1 slice protein toast with butter 9
coffee or tea (with/without heavy
    cream) 0-1

DINNER

steak (unlimited amount) 0
mushrooms in butter 3
spinach salad with bacon bits 5
¼ c. vanilla ice cream with one shot of creme
    de menthe or creme de cacao 14
1 glass dry red wine (claret, burgundy) .. 1
coffee or tea (with/without heavy cream) . 0-1

                      Total 58-60

Chapter 8

Virgo

V irgo and her sister sign Gemini are ruled by the planet Mercury, the great inquisitor. You are always questioning and wanting to learn more. Your symbol is the virgin maiden.

Virgos are pragmatic and practical. Organization and concentration characterize a Virgo. You were the child who always was arranging and rearranging your toys. You just love to see things in order. You cannot tolerate chaos. You usually use your organization skills to good advantage, but sometimes you need to be more creative. Using your imagination makes life more interesting and less frustrating. Don't be so predictable.

You're considered conscientious and competent. You like having a steady job. Because you're so diligent, you're usually asked to take on more responsibility. You're good at taking charge, and you're commended for doing a good job.

You enjoy reading self-help and how-to books. You like to keep abreast of the latest developments in your field. Your attention to detail is extraordinary, and you have the uncanny ability to recall all the material you read. Your reputation as a perfectionist precedes you. In most cases, you'd rather do the work yourself so you're sure it meets your standards. You've set high standards for yourself and those around you, and you're critical of whoever doesn't measure up.

Although you'd never intentionally hurt or offend someone, they may be put off by your approach. What they don't realize is you're much harder on yourself. Mercury, your ruling planet, can help you understand human behavior and teach you to be more tactful, if you'll just listen. It's hard for you to understand passion because you rarely experience it, but you do realize that's not true for everyone. So be considerate of other people's feelings.

You have a scientific sort of mind. You like to observe life and classify your observations. Virgos like to analyze everything. Nothing escapes comparison. Everybody knows you're intelligent, but you don't flaunt it. You'd rather be the power behind the throne. You like to control the action behind the scenes. Virgos tend to let others get the glory. You're not interested in recognition—you like the satisfaction of a job well done. You shouldn't be so reserved. Get what you deserve.

You only feel comfortable with a plan in hand. Even when you're organized, you can still be self-critical. Keep in mind that no one, not even a Virgo, can be perfect. Try to relax and take it easy.

Virgo rules the sixth house, which represents service to others, health, employees, and work. Getting an executive position is one of your top priorities. You rarely lose your temper, but when you do, it's usually because something wasn't done properly. You have no qualms about pointing out what's wrong and demanding satisfaction. You remain in control of yourself. Your cool, calm exterior inspires confidence.

Thrift, conservation, knowledge—those are your watch words. You're quick to recognize an opportunity and take advantage of it. You leave nothing to chance. You trust your judgments instead. Virgos are great at devising long-range plans. You make things happen.

Virgos are generous. You usually give far more than you receive. But like other people, you need love, sympathy, and understanding. Look around and you'll find people who'd love to lend a sympathetic ear. It's much easier to get through the bad times with a little help from your friends.

Virgos approach life in a practical way. You usually find it hard to relax. You worry about almost everything, including those things you can't control. One of your biggest worries is your health and the health of those you care about. Virgos usually enjoy good health, but overwork, lack of sleep, and tension can lower your resistance. To avoid getting sick, you should get plenty of rest, eat three meals a day, and work at a slower pace.

Friends and family are always welcome in your home. No matter what time they arrive, everything is always in its proper place. Your possessions reflect your good taste. You enjoy material things, but you're more interested in people. The very young and the very old will hold a special place in your heart.

Since Virgo rules health, there is little you don't know or won't find out about diet and nutrition. But too often Virgos don't put what they know into practice. You'd rather read about it than do it.

Because you're so very health-conscious, you normally do something about your weight before it becomes a problem. If you've gained weight, it's probably because of tension-induced overeating. When you overindulge, it's usually on sweets and starches. Sometimes you binge on "health food," thinking it has fewer calories. Although it's high in vitamins and minerals and low in additives and coloring, you must realize that it can also be very fattening.

Tension is your diet's biggest enemy. Tension can ruin not just your diet, it can harm your health. To avoid tension-related problems, cut down on the heavy fats and proteins that are hard to digest. Substitute chicken, veal, or fish for pork and beef. Eat more raw vegetables and fresh fruits that are high in iron, vitamins, and minerals. Eat more high calcium, low calorie whole grains and dairy products. A high protein, low carbohydrate diet has too many calories for Virgos, who burn fuel slowly.

With your natural talent for organization, balancing your diet will be as easy to you as balancing your budget. You'll do the sensible thing when it comes to taking care of your health. And if you don't know what the sensible thing is, then you'll find out in a hurry.

Donna typifies the organized, well-read, health-conscious Virgo. She has a pretty face, a soft, clear complexion, and a halo of ash blond locks. Despite all her assets, Donna has always had a weight problem. She knows more about physical and mental health than anyone I know. She encourages her family and friends to eat right and get enough exercise, but when she needs to lose weight, she relies on dieting alone because she hates to exercise.

Several years ago, Donna went on a strict diet. She started at 170 pounds and ended in a size 8. She didn't look like the same person. Being beautiful was a problem for this Virgo native. She felt guilty about having so many people compliment her on her appearance, but doesn't anymore.

Being overweight bothers a Virgo more than anyone else since Virgos strive for perfection. If you're a few pounds over-weight, you probably try to take them off immediately. You like to keep your weight at the recommended level.

Margaret is an example of a determined Virgo who did just that. She went from a pleasingly plump 165 pounds to a trim 135 pounds. This young, exotic-looking writer from Liverpool was once overweight.

In August 1970, as the sun returned to her first house (Virgo), Margaret began to gradually lose weight. Soon, she was the perfect weight for her 5' 7" frame. She now keeps a strict watch on her weight, and immediately cuts down her intake if the scale varies even the slightest bit.

Begin your diet on a Wednesday after the full moon. Skip the high protein/low carbohydrate diets and concentrate on counting calories. Include high fiber foods like bran and whole wheat to keep your digestive tract in good working order. Your diet will be more successful if you wait until your Virgo sun returns to your first house (on your birthday) or when the sun enters Capricorn (December 21-January 20). You'll find it so easy to diet during those times that you'll wonder why you didn't figure it out before. Don't begin your diet while the sun is in Libra (September 21-October 20) or when the sun enters Sagittarius (November 21-December 20). You may lose, but you'll have to wrench off each pound.

You're a creature of habit, although you do enjoy surprises. Since good health is based on good eating habits, develop a health routine. Keep an accurate, detailed list of what you eat and record the calories on your menu planner.

You're not fond of physical activity, but exercise is important in any weight loss program. Make exercise part of your daily routine. Work in your garden. Try golf in the warm months and racquetball in the winter. If you really can't stand the thought of exercise, take a walk or paint a picture. Just *do* something. A healthy body means a healthy mind.

The charts on the following pages will help you find the best time for *you* to lose weight. The easy-to-use astrological wheel has directions on setting up your chart by using your birthday. It shows you how to follow your sun's progress through your twelve houses. The Solar Transit Chart lets you record your weight loss as the sun moves from one house to the next. There is also a first week's menu that will allow you to include the foods you and your family love in your diet.

Familiarize yourself with the astrological wheel and the significance of each house as it pertains to the Virgo native.

The houses follow in a counterclockwise circle. Each house covers about a thirty-day period.

- When the Virgo sun transits your first house (Virgo), you want to enhance your appearance (weight loss).

- When the Virgo sun transits your second house (Libra), you want to indulge yourself (weight gain).

- When the Virgo sun transits your third house (Scorpio), you are better able to express your ideas.

- When the Virgo sun transits your fourth house (Sagittarius), you want to nurture yourself.

- When the Virgo sun transits your fifth house (Capricorn), you achieve more confidence in yourself, your appearance, and your abilities (weight loss).

- When the Virgo sun transits your sixth house (Aquarius), you become more interested in your health and working conditions.

- When the Virgo sun transits your seventh house (Pisces), you form new relationships and your interest in other people is renewed.

- When the Virgo sun transits your eighth house (Aries), you become more interested in the resources of others as they affect you.

- When the Virgo sun transits your ninth house (Taurus), you devise new plans for the future.

- When the Virgo sun transits your tenth house (Gemini), you want to move ahead with your career plans.

- When the Virgo sun transits your eleventh house (Cancer), you want to cooperate in a group effort.

- When the Virgo sun transits your twelfth house (Leo), you discover information previously unavailable to you.

- As the sun leaves your twelfth house and prepares to enter your first house again, you will be given a chance to reassess your last solar year and lay plans for the new year ahead.

To personalize your solar wheel, insert your birthdate (month and day) in the blank space marked number 1 Virgo. Then, moving counterclockwise, insert the next month and same day in the blank space marked 2 Libra. Continue around the solar wheel, marking the month and day in the blank spaces, until you come full circle.

You will now be able to follow the sun's transits through your horoscope and anticipate what areas of your life will be highlighted each thirty-day period. The transits will also tell you the times during the year dieting will be most successful. For those people who are born on the cusp of a sign (three days before or three days after), refer to the Solar Position Chart to find out what your sun sign really is.

To see how one dieter personalized his solar wheel, see page 29.

Solar Wheel Chart

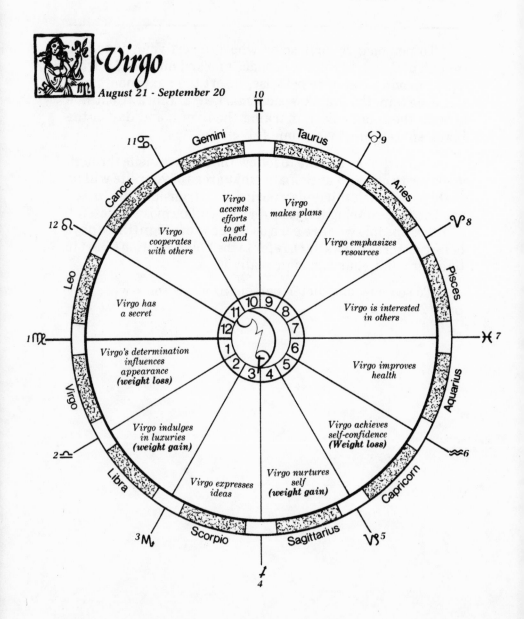

Virgo
August 21 - September 20

10
Ⅱ

11 ♋ Gemini Taurus ♉ 9

Cancer Aries

12 ♌ Virgo accents efforts to get ahead Virgo makes plans ♈ 8

Leo Virgo cooperates with others Virgo emphasizes resources Pisces

1 ♍ Virgo has a secret 11 10 9 8 7 Virgo is interested in others ♓ 7

Virgo's determination influences appearance *(weight loss)* 12 6 Virgo improves health

Virgo 1 5
2 3 4 5

Virgo indulges in luxuries *(weight gain)* Virgo achieves self-confidence *(Weight loss)* Aquarius

2 ♎ Libra ♒ 6

Virgo expresses ideas Virgo nurtures self *(weight gain)* Capricorn

3 ♏ Scorpio Sagittarius ♑ 5

♐
4

100 *Diet Signs*

The Solar Transit Chart provides you with a guide to those times of the year when you will lose weight and those times you will gain weight.

Insert your birthdate (month and day) at the top of the chart in the space marked number 1 Virgo. Then insert the next month and same day in the space marked number 2 Libra. Continue across the top of the page until you reach 12 Leo.

Record your total weight loss or gain with an X. At the end of the solar year, connect the Xs to reveal your astrological pattern.

To see how one dieter recorded her weight, see page 31.

Virgo Solar Transit Chart

House Numbers, Signs and Corresponding Dates

Lbs.	Virgo	Libra	Scorpio	Sagittarius	Capricorn	Aquarius.	Pisces	Aries	Taurus	Gemini	Cancer	Leo
10												
9												
8												
7												
6												
5												
4												
3												
2												
1												
-1												
-2												
-3												
-4												
-5												
-6												
-7												
-8												
-9												
-10												

Start your diet with this low calorie menu. It allows 1200 calories for women and 1500 calories for men. Never skip a meal. Enjoy each one. Check substitutions in the calorie/carbohydrate/protein counter in Appendix C. Once you've planned your diet, don't deviate from your mealtime routine much. Before starting this or any other diet, check with your doctor to be sure your weight gain isn't caused by some physical condition. Recipes for some of the suggested dishes (marked with an asterisk) in your menu appear in Chapter 15.

Virgo: First Week's Menu

Day One: Wednesday

BREAKFAST | Calories
½ papaya .... | 60
1 piece French toast (1 tsp. maple syrup) . | 175
1 cup coffee or tea (with/without skim
    milk and 1 tsp. sugar)................. | 0-25

LUNCH
1 c. chicken noodle soup .... | 65
chef salad (lettuce, tomato, 1 slice cheese,
    1 oz. ham, 1 hard-boiled egg, and 1 tbsp.
    diet dressing)......................... | 315
1 cup coffee or tea (with/without skim milk
    and 1 tsp. sugar), diet soda, water ..... | 0-25

DINNER
½ c. raw spinach salad (1 strip cooked
    bacon and 1 tbsp. diet dressing) .... | 91
4 oz. chicken .... | 200
½ c. instant rice .... | 71
½ c. yellow squash steamed with 1
    pat butter .... | 50
ambrosia............................... | 101
1 cup coffee or tea (with/without skim
    milk and 1 tsp. sugar), diet soda, water | 0-25

Total | 1128-1203

Day Two: Thursday

BREAKFAST Calories

½ grapefruit with ½ tbsp. honey.......... 85
1 c. puffed wheat or puffed rice (½ c. skim
   milk and 1 tsp. sugar)................. 110
1 cup coffee or tea (with/without skim
   milk and 1 tsp. sugar)................. 0-25

LUNCH

⅓ c. cottage cheese with ½ c. fresh fruit on
   lettuce leaf 110
blueberry muffin and 1 pat butter 176
1 cup coffee or tea (with/without skim
   milk and 1 tsp. sugar), diet soda, water 0-25

DINNER

cube steak with peppers and tomatoes.... 260
½ c. mashed potatoes 100
½ c. broccoli steamed with herbs 20
2 small cookies 100
1 cup coffee or tea (with/without skim
   milk and 1 tsp. sugar), diet soda, water 0-25

                                  Total   961-
                                              1036

Day Three: Friday

BREAKFAST Calories

8 oz. orange juice....................... 120
1 egg cooked any way 100
1 slice of toast with 1 pat butter.......... 106
1 cup of coffee or tea (with/without skim
   milk and 1 tsp. sugar)................. 0-25

LUNCH

California tuna salad* 200
lettuce leaf............................. 5
1 dill pickle 10
treat (your choice) 80
1 cup coffee or tea (with/without skim milk
   and 1 tsp. sugar), diet soda, water 0-25

DINNER

beef stew	240
lettuce and tomato salad (1 tbsp. diet dressing)*	60
dessert peaches.........................	50
1 glass lite beer	80
1 cup coffee or tea (with/without skim milk and 1 tsp. sugar), diet soda, water	0-25
Total	1051-1126

Day Four: Saturday

BREAKFAST
Calories

8 oz. orange juice.......................	120
carob drink*	88
1 cup coffee or tea (with/without skim milk and 1 tsp. sugar).....................	0-25

LUNCH

4 oz. steamed shrimp on lettuce	108
1 c. Manhattan clam chowder	81
1 apple	61
1 cup coffee or tea (with/without skim milk and 1 tsp. sugar), diet soda, water	0-25

DINNER

½ 10" cheese pizza......................	500
salad with 1 tbsp. diet dressing	60
1 glass lite beer, diet soda, water........	0-80
Total	968-1148

Day Five: Sunday

BREAKFAST
Calories

eggs benedict (1 serving)	296
fruit salad	126
1 cup coffee or tea (with/without skim milk and 1 tsp. sugar).................	0-25

LUNCH

1 lb. lobster with 1 tbsp. butter	212
4 oz. steak	235
½ baked potato with 1 pat butter (or 1 tbsp. sour cream and chives)................	111
salad with 1 tbsp. diet dressing	60
1 glass wine, diet soda, water	0-90
1 cup coffee or tea (with/without skim milk and 1 tsp. sugar).................	0-25

DINNER

1 open-face melted cheese sandwich with tomato	185
½ c. tomato soup	55
1 cup coffee or tea (with/without skim milk and 1 tsp. sugar), diet soda, water	0-25
Total	1280-1445

Day Six: Monday

BREAKFAST

Calories

½ small cantaloupe	58
1 slice toast with 1 pat butter	106
1 cup coffee or tea (with/without skim milk and 1 tsp. sugar).................	0-25

LUNCH

egg salad sandwich with 1 tbsp. mayonnaise and lettuce leaf	310
celery sticks	10
carrot sticks	21
1 small cookie..........................	50
1 cup coffee or tea (with/without skim milk and 1 tsp. sugar), diet soda, water	0-25

DINNER

Hawaiian chicken	181
2 oz. spaghetti, oriental style.............	210
lettuce wedge with 1 tbsp. diet dressing ..	40
½ c. zucchini	55
1 glass chianti, diet soda, water	0-100
Total	1041-1191

Day Seven: Tuesday

BREAKFAST

	Calories
8 oz. unsweetened grapefruit juice	101
1 c. *Special K* cereal (½ c. skim milk and 1 tsp. sugar)	129
coffee or tea (with/without skim milk and 1 tsp. sugar)	0-25

LUNCH

McDonald's cheeseburger	306
small french fries	211
coffee or tea (with/without skim milk and 1 tsp. sugar), diet soda, water	0-25

DINNER

8 oz. flounder	180
½ c. cole slaw	60
½ c. steamed carrots and 1 pat butter and herbs	59
½ cantaloupe	58
coffee or tea (with/without skim milk and 1 tsp. sugar), diet soda, water	0-25
Total	1104-1179

Chapter 9

Libra

Libra is represented by the scales of justice. Natives of this sign are ruled by Venus, which governs personal relationships, beauty, music, literature, and art. The primary relationships that concern all Librans are marriage and partnerships. Because of their interest in relationships, Librans make the best public relations people and diplomats.

Librans are very exceptional people. They can usually be found negotiating contracts or settling a quarrel between two squabbling children. Librans abound in professions where tact and diplomacy are essential. They have the ability to see both sides of an argument. Librans should take pride in their justly deserved reputation for fairness. A Libra native can be counted on to give an honest evaluation.

Librans love to please, and people love to be around you. You're genuinely interested in people, and you know how to make them feel important. You're truly one of life's "beautiful people"—for your tact, your fairness, and your ability to get along with everyone.

Your home is always the scene of much activity. You entertain in style. You make your guests feel welcome. Your gatherings are known for the interesting, fun people you invite. Your home is open to friends and strangers alike. You believe that every stranger is a potential friend, and you make friends easily.

You exude the charm Venus endowed you with. Most people succumb to it sooner or later, and it's usually sooner. You hate to feel left out, and because of your winning ways, you rarely are. Others go out of their way to please you, because you're witty, vivacious, and fun to be around. If things seem too quiet, you'll call up a few friends for a night on the town.

Achieving balance and beauty are among your main concerns. Your sign represents the artists and musicians. As a connoisseur of the finer things in life, you take great pleasure in surrounding yourself with beautiful objects and beautiful people. Looking attractive, knowing the right thing to wear, say, or do—it comes as easily as breathing. You were born with a natural elegance that makes you special. If you can't afford to buy what you want, you harness your creativity to make something infinitely better. All Librans have that touch of class.

You've got so much going for you that people find it hard to believe you ever have problems. As the great arbitrator of the zodiac, you are often asked to help others reach a decision. But, when it comes to your life, you sometimes have trouble making up your mind. Once the decision is made, you may still agonize whether it was the right one. You should learn to quit worrying about what's over and done with.

You dislike being alone. You see life in terms of partnerships. People usually seek you out. People are always coming to you with their problems, and you always manage to find time for them. You are usually the strongest partner in any relationship. You'll go to great lengths to keep a relationship together. But, in some instances, you might be asked to give just too much. Know when this is happening and as hard as it might be, it may be better to let that person go. There are so many people in the world who would cherish and value your friendship highly and you should never have to settle for less.

Venus rules the sweet things in life—including candy, ice cream, and pastries. Your sweet tooth makes it hard for you to diet. What, not how much, you eat is usually the problem. You'd much rather eat cake and forsake the vegetables. You're the person who can't eat just one. You couldn't stick to any diet that didn't allow you to indulge your sweet tooth. So I won't ask you to do it. I will ask you to cut down, though.

Use the whole grain products like oatmeal bread instead of white bread. If you have to use sugar, switch to honey, molasses, real maple syrup, or a sugar substitute (e.g., fructose). Substitute fresh raspberries and cream or cantaloupe sprinkled with fresh (or frozen) blueberries for pastry. If you need a sweet pick-me-up at the end of a meal, have Irish coffee or a capuccino. Most diet books will tell you to leave the high calorie sweets alone, but we both know that this is impossible for you, so save it until the final hour and then indulge yourself in a small sweet and don't feel guilty.

Before you begin this or any diet, check the Desirable Weight Chart in Appendix A to see what you should weigh. Then check with your doctor to see if you really need to lose weight. He or she can be objective. Some Librans actually have a weight problem, but many more only think they do. Most Librans weigh exactly what they should. But they might not believe it if they feel their body is out of proportion. It may be hard for you to accept what other people tell you—that you don't need to diet. If you are overweight, you may also find it hard to believe that people could love you in spite of your weight. If your appearance bothers you, just cut down on your calorie intake. You're much harsher on yourself than anyone else would be.

If you've decided to start your diet, think about dieting with a friend. Encourage and counsel each other on the best diets, new recipes, and calorie-cutting tricks. Forgive each other for occasionally going off your diet. It isn't the end of the world if you slip up once in a while. Don't feel guilty, just get right back on your diet. If you feel a binge coming on, call your diet buddy for moral support.

Dorothy, an attractive, sophisticated Libran, has perfected the buddy system. Whenever Dorothy decides to start a diet, she manages to get most of her friends involved. She then becomes their inspiration. Dorothy joined a diet group in October, as the sun entered her first house. She lost twelve pounds in the first ten weeks, restyled her hair, and bought a new, more flattering wardrobe.

Librans have a talent for bringing people together. It might be fun to start a volleyball team, or organize a badminton tournament in your neighborhood. Librans are also terrific dancers. Consider taking or teaching an aerobic dance class. If exercise doesn't appeal to you at all, then visit a large art gallery where you have to do a lot of walking.

To keep you on the straight and narrow where diets are concerned, get together with your special friend and have an elegant dinner at home using the latest low-calorie French recipes. Try an exotic lunch at a good restaurant: start with consomme, then order a fresh salad, move on to plain, unadorned meat with fresh, steamed vegetables, sip a glass of dry red or white wine, and finish the meal with a slice of fresh pineapple and an orange capuccino. You Librans appreciate the finer things in life, and a diet dinner with a friend or an elegant low-calorie lunch will help you stick to your diet.

The best times for you to begin to diet are when the sun transits through Libra on your birthday, or when the sun enters Aquarius (January 21-February 20). If you start your diet when the sun is in Scorpio (October 21-November 20) or Capricorn (December 21-January 20), you'll find each pound a struggle. That can be discouraging. Don't begin your diet until the Friday after the full moon. Otherwise, you may retain fluid. Don't fall for the latest fad diets and try not to skip breakfast.

Rather than being overweight, you may simply have a

weight distribution problem. If that's the case, exercise is the solution. Carol Ann fits this description. She worked as a registered nurse in a demanding job. But when she moved four years ago, she started gaining weight in the wrong places, and it refused to come off. When we met again, Carol Ann looked terrific. I asked her how she did it. Her secret was: eat less after 2:00 p.m., and exercise at a nearby health spa. That way she could easily control her weight.

The charts on the following pages will help you find the best time for *you* to lose weight. The easy-to-use astrological wheel has directions on setting up your chart by using your birthday. It shows you how to follow your sun's progress through your twelve houses. The Solar Transit Chart lets you record your weight loss as the sun moves from one house to the next. There is also a first week's menu that will allow you to include the foods you and your family love in your diet.

Familiarize yourself with the astrological wheel and the significance of each house as it pertains to the native. The houses follow in a counterclockwise circle. Each house covers about a thirty-day period.

- When the Libra sun transits your first house (Libra), you want to enhance your appearance (weight loss).

- When the Libra sun transits your second house (Scorpio), you want to indulge yourself (weight gain).

- When the Libra sun transits your third house (Sagittarius), you are better able to express your ideas.

- When the Libra sun transits your fourth house (Capricorn), you want to nurture yourself (weight gain).

- When the Libra sun transits your fifth house (Aquarius), you achieve more confidence in yourself, your appearance, and your abilities (weight loss).

- When the Libra sun transits your sixth house (Pisces),

you become more interested in your health and working conditions.

- When the Libra sun transits your seventh house (Aries), you form new relationships and your interest in others is renewed.

- When the Libra sun transits your eighth house (Taurus), you become interested in the resources of others as they affect you.

- When the Libra sun transits your ninth house (Gemini), you devise new plans for the future.

- When the Libra sun transits your tenth house (Cancer), you move ahead with your career plans.

- When the Libra sun transits your eleventh house (Leo), you want to cooperate with other people in a group effort.

- When the Libra sun transits your twelfth house (Virgo), you discover information previously unavailable to you.

- As the sun leaves your twelfth house and prepares to enter your first house again, you will be given a chance to reassess your last solar year and lay plans for the new year ahead.

To personalize your solar wheel insert your birthdate (month and day) in the blank space marked number 1 Libra. Then, moving counterclockwise, insert the next month and same day in the blank space marked number 2 Scorpio. Continue around the solar wheel marking the month and day in the blank spaces until you come full circle.

You will now be able to follow the sun's transits through your horoscope and anticipate what areas of your life will be highlighted each thirty-day period. The transits will also tell you the times during the year dieting will be most successful. For those people born on the cusp of a sign (three days before or three days after) refer to the Solar Position Chart to find out what your sun sign really is.

To see how one dieter personalized his solar wheel, see page 29.

Solar Wheel Chart

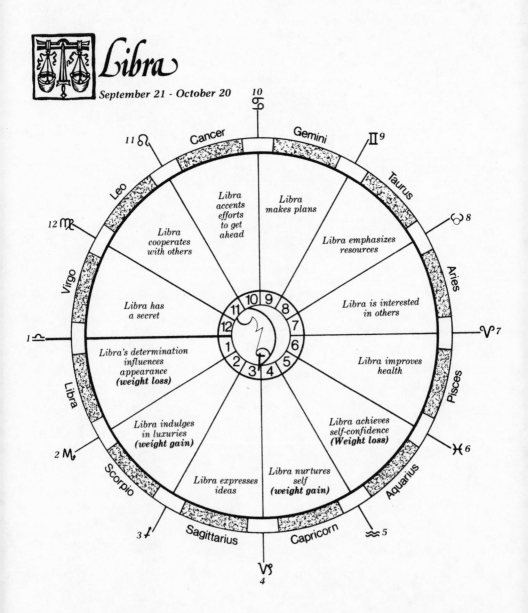

𝓛ibra

September 21 - October 20

10 ♋

11 ♌   Cancer   Gemini   ♊ 9

Leo   Taurus

Libra accents efforts to get ahead

Libra makes plans

12 ♍   Libra cooperates with others   ♉ 8

Virgo   Aries

Libra emphasizes resources

Libra has a secret

Libra is interested in others

1 ♎   11 10 9 8   ♈ 7

12   7

1   6

2 3 4 5

Libra's determination influences appearance **(weight loss)**

Libra improves health

Libra   Pisces

Libra indulges in luxuries **(weight gain)**

Libra achieves self-confidence **(Weight loss)**

2 ♏   ♓ 6

Scorpio   Aquarius

Libra expresses ideas

Libra nurtures self **(weight gain)**

Aquarius

3 ♐   Sagittarius   Capricorn   ♒ 5

♑
4

The Solar Transit Chart provides you with a guide to those times of the year when you will lose weight and those times you will gain weight.

Insert your birthdate at the top of the chart in the space marked number 1 Libra. Then insert the next month and same day in the space marked number 2 Scorpio. Continue across the top of the page until you reach 12 Virgo.

Record your total weight loss or gain with an X. At the end of the solar year, connect the Xs to reveal your astrological pattern.

To see how one dieter recorded her weight, see page 31.

Libra Solar Transit Chart

House Numbers, Signs and Corresponding Dates

Lbs.	Libra	Scorpio	Sagittarius	Capricorn	Aquarius	Pisces	Aries	Taurus	Gemini	Cancer	Leo	Virgo
10												
9												
8												
7												
6												
5												
4												
3												
2												
1												
-1												
-2												
-3												
-4												
-5												
-6												
-7												
-8												
-9												
-10												

I've outlined a week's worth of menus, allotting 1200 calories for women and 1500 calories for men. Once you've dieted to your recommended weight, gradually increase your calories until you find a level where you can maintain your weight. Check substitutions or exchanges in the calorie/carbohydrate/protein counter in Appendix C. Recipes for some of the suggested dishes (marked with an asterisk) are in Chapter 15.

Libra: First Week's Menu

Day One: Friday

	Calories
BREAKFAST	
1 c. oatmeal (with ½ c. skim milk and 1 tsp. sugar)	195
1 cup coffee or tea (with/without skim milk and 1 tsp. sugar)	0-25
SNACK	
1 orange	65
1 slice whole wheat toast and 1 pat butter	101
4 oz. skim milk	45
LUNCH	
2 tacos	360
diet soda, mineral water, water	0-25
SNACK	
½ c. yogurt with ½ c. strawberries	65
herbal tea	0
DINNER	
egg omelette with mushrooms and 1 slice cooked bacon	270
lettuce and tomato salad with 1 tbsp. diet dressing	60
iced herbal tea, mineral water, water	0-25
SNACK	
1 cup chicken bouillon	20
2 saltine crackers	25
Total	1206-1281

Day Two: Saturday

BREAKFAST Calories
½ small cantaloupe 60
1 cup coffee or tea (with/without skim
   milk and 1 tsp. sugar)................. 0-25

SNACK
4 oz. orange juice....................... 60
corn muffin and 1 pat butter 166

LUNCH
4 oz. shrimp salad 210
1 c. chicken with rice soup.............. 45
diet soda, mineral water, water 0-25

SNACK
carrot, zucchini, and cucumber chips..... 41
4 oz. vegetable juice 20

DINNER
lamb curry............................. 290
½ c. noodles 100
lettuce and tomato salad with 1 tbsp. diet
   dressing............................. 60
iced herbal tea, mineral water, water 0-25

SNACK
½ apple 35
1 oz. swiss cheese...................... 105
1 cup herbal tea........................ 0-25

Total 1192-
1292

Day Three: Sunday

BREAKFAST Calories
6 oz. grapefruit juice 75
1 slice french toast (1 tsp. maple syrup) .. 175
1 cup coffee or tea (with/without skim
   milk and 1 tsp. sugar)................. 0-25

SNACK
½ c. fresh strawberries 20
8 oz. skim milk......................... 90

LUNCH

½ c. plain cottage cheese with tomato on lettuce leaf	130
1 hard cooked egg	82
diet soda, mineral water, water	0-25

SNACK

1 oz. cheese and 4 saltine crackers	160
1 glass dry wine.......................	85

DINNER

4 oz. broiled sole filet....................	80
4 stalks asparagus with herb or lemon juice	10
spaghetti squash with 1 pat butter	100
iced herb tea, mineral water, water	0-25

SNACK

baked apple...........................	130
herbal tea............................	0-25
Total	1137-1237

Day Four: Monday

BREAKFAST
Calories

1 blueberry muffin with 1 pat butter.....	176
coffee or tea (with/without skim milk and 1 tsp. sugar)	0-25

SNACK

4 oz. orange juice......................	60
fruit salad	126

LUNCH

3½ oz. shrimp with cocktail sauce	125
½ c. Manhattan style clam chowder	35
diet soda, mineral water, water	0-25

SNACK

celery sticks	10
carrot sticks	21
radishes	5
dip	30
4 oz. vegetable juice	20

DINNER

steak and tomatoes*	260
meaty rice*	120
lettuce and tomato salad with 1 tbsp. diet dressing*	60
iced herbal tea, mineral water, water	0-25

SNACK

strawberry shortcake	140
decaffeinated coffee or herbal tea (with/without skim milk and 1 tsp. sugar)	0-25
Total	1188-1288

Day Five: Tuesday

BREAKFAST

	Calories
hot lemonade	35
1 slice whole wheat toast and 1 pat butter	101
1 cup coffee or tea (with/without skim milk and 1 tsp. sugar)	0-25

SNACK

5 dried apricots or 3 fresh apricots	55
4 oz. skim milk	45

LUNCH

McDonald's cheeseburger	306
diet soda, mineral water, water	0-25

SNACK

zucchini and cucumber chips	20
cherry tomatoes	20
herbal tea	0-25

DINNER

½ 10" cheese pizza	500
salad and 1 tbsp. diet dressing	60
iced herbal tea, mineral water, water	0-25

SNACK

pineapple yogurt shake	135
Total	1277-1377

Day Six: Wednesday

	Calories
BREAKFAST	
1 egg cooked any way	100
1 cup coffee or tea (with/without skim milk and 1 tsp. sugar).................	0-25
SNACK	
1 small apple...........................	80
4 oz. orange juice.......................	60
LUNCH	
spinach salad	160
diet soda, mineral water, water	0-25
SNACK	
1 bran muffin and 1 pat butter	136
1 cup coffee or tea (with/without skim milk and 1 tsp. sugar).................	0-25
DINNER	
stir-fry broccoli beef....................	289
½ c. instant rice	71
½ c. steamed carrots and herbs	20
iced herbal tea, mineral water, water	0-25
SNACK	
2 small fig cookies......................	100
6 oz. lite cocoa	70
Total	1086-1186

Day Seven: Thursday

	Calories
BREAKFAST	
1 c. puffed wheat or puffed rice (½ c. skim milk and 1 tsp. sugar).................	110
1 cup coffee or tea (with/without skim milk and 1 tsp. sugar).................	0-25
SNACK	
Hawaiian breakfast drink	96

LUNCH

open-face melted cheese sandwich with
   tomato 185
celery sticks 10
carrot sticks 21
diet soda, mineral water, water 0-25

SNACK

¼ cantaloupe 30
6 oz. apple cider...................... 90

DINNER

4 oz. lamb chop 240
½ c. broccoli and herbs 25
½ yam baked with 1 pat butter 116
lettuce and tomato salad with 1 tbsp.
   diet dressing....................... 60
iced herb tea, mineral water, water 0-25

SNACK

individual cheesecake................... 170
decaffeinated coffee or herbal tea (with/
   without skim milk and 1 tsp. sugar) ... 0-25

TOTAL   1148-
1223

Chapter 10

Scorpio

Scorpio is the only sign that has co-rulers. Mars, the God of War, was originally your ruler, but when Pluto was discovered, astrologers thought it was a good vehicle to express the sign of Scorpio. There are four symbols of your power: the scorpion, the eagle, the phoenix, and the serpent of wisdom. Is it any wonder that Scorpio is considered the most powerful sign in the zodiac? You have the ability to display any one of Scorpio's attributes at any given time. Your sign rules the eighth house—resources, regeneration, high finance, and the occult.

You're considered the passionate sign of the zodiac. Although you are sexy, your passion extends mainly to your quest for knowledge. You love to learn, and you realize that knowledge is power.

Scorpio natives tend to lead active social lives. Your mystic quality exerts an almost hypnotic fascination. No one can be indifferent to a Scorpio native. Your ability to see through people amazes them. It can be unnerving for some people. Scorpios are not game players. To them, life is a very serious business. Nothing that Scorpio wants to learn can be kept from him or her for long.

You're extremely creative, but you don't feel that you are since it's part of your nature. Scorpios are great pretenders. You appear calm, cool, and detached, even when you're not. Scorpio natives are so secretive, even those who think they know you best don't really know you. The word of a Scorpio is never given lightly, and they don't like to be crossed. Scorpio never forgets: they are good allies or fearsome enemies. Scorpio doesn't get revenge, he just gets even. As a friend, he is one of the most loyal and the most powerful. He will never forget a kindness and he will repay that kindness tenfold.

Scorpio is a fixed water sign represented by ice. Scorpios are patient seekers. You were a loner as a child, and you're still that way. You were the one who always wanted to know why. You asked and still asked questions for a reason—you needed the answers to survive. Even as a child, you had great powers of concentration that enabled you to size up a situation or person quickly. You valued adults when you were young, very highly, especially the ones who took the time to teach you something.

Unlike your graceful sister sign Libra, you are the mechanic of the zodiac. You cloak yourself in mystery. You're usually so engrossed in what you're doing that you don't have time to explain yourself to anyone else. You're probably the most controlled sign in the zodiac. One of Scorpio's biggest fears is letting go.

The will power of Scorpio natives colors everything they do. You can stick to a diet if you put your mind to it. If you think dieting will enhance your power or lead to a new insight, you'll do it. Strangely enough, in some Scorpios, especially male Scorpios, being overweight can be an advantage. Size can be intimidating. Those Scorpios may feel that by losing weight they'll lose respect. Scorpio women usually see it differently. If a Scorpio woman feels overweight and unattractive, she'll go on a diet—as simple as that. In six months she'll be a different woman. Most Scorpios are in good health, but you tend to overdo when it comes to food, wine, and sex. The passionate eating scenes in the movie "Tom Jones" had to have been inspired by a Scorpio native.

You diet quietly. Most people don't even know you have a weight problem. You like to devise little ways of cutting calories, like ordering a Perrier with a twist, trimming the fat from your meat, or eating only a small part of your baked potato. You like rich, spicy foods washed down with an excellent bottle of wine. While on your diet, try to substitute fish and shellfish for meats.

When you do gain a few extra pounds, don't worry. You're one of the water signs, so it should come off easily. The best times to rid yourself of unwanted weight are before the holidays, when the sun is in Scorpio (October 21-November 20), and at the end of the astrological calendar, when the sun is in Pisces (February 21-March 20). If you can avoid it, don't start your diet while the sun is in Sagittarius (November 21-December 20) or when the sun enters Aquarius (January 21-February 20). Those holiday parties can do you in. Always start your diet on the Tuesday after the full moon.

If you think I'm joking about the moon, let me tell you about Martha. She's a fascinating New Mexican Scorpio with flashing dark eyes and a quick laugh. She cooks rich, spicy dishes with all the passion of her sign. Despite her delicious cooking, Martha usually stays her normal weight except once a month, when she'd notice a distinct tightness in some of her clothes. I studied her chart, and like all water signs, Martha gained weight as the moon waxed and lost weight as the moon waned.

You too may find, as Rosa my bilingual secretary from Honduras did, that many times you do not even have to diet consciously. When the sun is positioned in your first and fifth house you may lose those few extra pounds overnight with no fuss or bother. And that, my friend, is what you are aiming for. You want to lose weight as easily and as fast as possible, but always keep in mind that you want to do it the healthy way, so that it will stay off permanently.

Unlike Virgo, you hate anything routine. So for you exercise has to be fun and challenging. "Live for today, for tomorrow we die," is the motto you live by. Once you master a sport, the excitement is gone and you move on. The best place for you to exercise is in the water or on the ice—perhaps snow skiing in the winter and water skiing in the summer, or ice skating in the winter and white water rafting in the summer. And, knowing Scorpio as I do, when you have mastered all the other traditional sports, you will turn any challenge into a sport or create a new one.

The charts on the following pages will help you find the best time for *you* to lose weight. The easy-to-use astrological wheel has directions on setting up your chart by using your birthday. It shows you how to follow your sun's progress through your twelve houses. The Solar Transit Chart lets you record your weight loss as the sun moves from one house to the next. There is also a first week's menu that will allow you to include the foods you and your family love in your diet.

Familiarize yourself with the astrological wheel and the significance of each house as it pertains to the Scorpio native. The houses follow in a counterclockwise circle. Each house covers about a thirty-day period.

- When the Scorpio sun transits your first house (Scorpio), you want to enhance your appearance (weight loss).

- When the Scorpio sun transits your second house (Sagittarius), you want to indulge yourself (weight gain).

- When the Scorpio sun transits your third house (Capricorn), you are better able to express your ideas.

- When the Scorpio sun transits your fourth house (Aquarius), you want to nurture yourself (weight gain).

- When the Scorpio sun transits your fifth house (Pisces), you achieve more confidence in yourself, your appearance, and your abilities (weight loss).

- When the Scorpio sun transits your sixth house (Aries), you become more interested in your health and working conditions.

- When the Scorpio sun transits your seventh house (Taurus), you form new relationships and your interest in others is renewed.

- When the Scorpio sun transits your eighth house (Gemini), you become interested in the resources of others as they affect you.

- When the Scorpio sun transits your ninth house (Cancer), you devise new plans for the future.

- When the Scorpio sun transits your tenth house (Leo), you move ahead with your career plans.

- When the Scorpio sun transits your eleventh house (Virgo), you want to cooperate in a group effort.

- When the Scorpio sun transits your twelfth house (Libra), you discover information previously unavailable to you.

- As the sun leaves your twelfth house and prepares to enter your first house again, you will be given a chance to reassess your last solar year and lay plans for the new year ahead.

To personalize your solar wheel insert your birthdate (month and day) in the blank space marked number 1 Scorpio. Then moving counterclockwise, insert the next month and same day in the blank space marked number 2 Sagittarius. Continue around the solar wheel marking the month and day in the blank spaces until you come full circle.

You will now be able to follow the sun's transits through your horoscope and anticipate what areas of your life will be highlighted each thirty-day period. The transits will also tell you the times during the year dieting will be most successful. For those people born on the cusp of a sign (three days before or three days after) refer to the Solar Position Chart to find out what your sun really is.

To see how one dieter personalized his solar wheel, see page 29.

Solar Wheel Chart

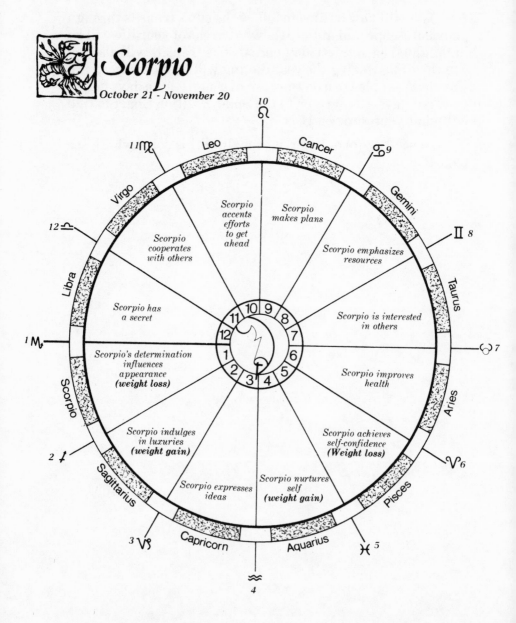

Scorpio
October 21 - November 20

10
♌

11 ♍   Leo   Cancer   ♋ 9

Virgo   Gemini

12 ♎   Ⅱ 8

Libra   Taurus

Scorpio accents efforts to get ahead

Scorpio makes plans

Scorpio cooperates with others

Scorpio emphasizes resources

Scorpio has a secret

Scorpio is interested in others

1 ♏   ♋ 7

Scorpio's determination influences appearance **(weight loss)**

Scorpio improves health

Scorpio

Aries

Scorpio indulges in luxuries **(weight gain)**

Scorpio achieves self-confidence **(Weight loss)**

2 ♐   ♈ 6

Sagittarius

Scorpio expresses ideas

Scorpio nurtures self **(weight gain)**

Pisces

3 ♑   Capricorn   Aquarius   ♓ 5

≈
4

The Solar Transit Chart provides you with a guide to those times of the year when you will lose weight and those times you will gain weight.

Insert your birthdate at the top of the chart in the space marked number 1 Scorpio. Then insert the next month and same day in the space marked number 2 Sagittarius. Continue across the top of the page until you reach 12 Libra.

Record your total weight loss or gain with an X. At the end of the solar year, connect the Xs to reveal your astrological pattern.

To see how one dieter recorded her weight, see page 31.

Scorpio Solar Transit Chart

House Numbers, Signs and Corresponding Dates

Lbs.	Scorpio	Sagittarius	Capricorn	Aquarius	Pisces	Aries	Taurus	Gemini	Cancer	Leo	Virgo	Libra
10												
9												
8												
7												
6												
5												
4												
3												
2												
1												
-1												
-2												
-3												
-4												
-5												
-6												
-7												
-8												
-9												
-10												

The menu I recommend starts with a liquid diet to shrink your stomach. Do not stay on it for more than twenty-four hours. It's a good way to flush out your system and get rid of excess water weight. Keep fluid retention problems to a minimum by drinking plenty of water. Besides, it's great for your complexion. After your one-day liquid diet, you will use a low-calorie diet (1200 calories for women, 1500 calories for men). Check substitutions and exchanges with the calorie/carbohydrate/protein counter in Appendix C. Be sure to check with your doctor before starting this or any other diet.

Scorpio: First Day's Menu

Day One: Tuesday

BREAKFAST
vegetable juice (any kind)
8 oz. milk
1 cup coffee or tea (with/without skim milk
    and 1 tsp. sugar), water

LUNCH
tomato soup
1 cup coffee or tea (with/without skim milk
    and 1 tsp. sugar), diet soda, water

DINNER
fruit soup*
vegetable juice (any kind)
jello made with fruit juice and topped with
    1 tbsp. cream
1 cup coffee or tea (with/without skim milk
    and 1 tsp. sugar), diet soda, water

Only use this menu once. Any amount of juice, liquid, or soup can be substituted for items on the menu.

*See Chapter 15

Scorpio: First Week's Menu

Day Two: Wednesday

BREAKFAST Calories

½ c. oatmeal (with ½ c. skim milk plus
   1 tsp. sugar) 104
8 oz. orange juice........................ 120
1 cup coffee or tea (with/without skim
   milk and 1 tsp. sugar)................. 0-25

LUNCH

1 cup clam chowder 100
lettuce and tomato salad (1 tbsp.
   diet dressing)........................ 60
1 apple and 1 oz. cheese 180
iced tea, coffee, diet soda, water.......... 0-25

DINNER

spicy shrimp* 245
½ c. instant rice 90
½ c. carrots and 1 pat butter............. 60
¼ cantaloupe cut into chunks with ½ c.
   fresh strawberries and 2 oz. vanilla
   ice cream............................. 125
1 cup coffee or tea (with/without skim milk
   and 1 tsp. sugar), diet soda, water 0-25

Total   1084-
1159

Day Three: Thursday

BREAKFAST Calories

6 oz. cranberry juice 123
1 egg cooked any way 100
1 slice of toast and 1 pat butter 100
1 cup coffee or tea (with/without skim
   milk and 1 tsp. sugar)................. 0-25

LUNCH

½ c. tuna salad with fruit or vegetables... 200
2 saltine crackers 25
iced tea, coffee, diet soda, water.......... 0-25

DINNER

1 c. macaroni and cheese	430
½ c. fresh steamed broccoli with 1 pat butter	55
lettuce wedge (1 tbsp. diet dressing)......	30
coffee or tea (with/without skim milk and 1 tsp. sugar), diet soda, water	0-25
Total	1063-1138

Day Four: Friday

BREAKFAST

Calories

¼ cantaloupe	40
yogurt shake	135
coffee or tea (with/without skim milk and 1 tsp. sugar)	0-25

LUNCH

openface turkey sandwich	185
1 tbsp. cranberry sauce.................	25
lettuce and tomato salad (1 tbsp. diet dressing)	60
dessert (your choice)....................	200
iced tea, coffee, diet soda, water..........	0-25

DINNER

New England style fish..................	180
1 baked potato with 1 pat butter	110
mixed fresh vegetables, steamed	45
1 fried banana and 1 tsp. whipped cream	145
coffee or tea (with/without skim milk and 1 tsp. sugar), diet soda, water	0-25
Total	1125-1200

Day Five: Saturday

BREAKFAST

Calories

openface cheese sandwich on 1 slice whole wheat bread	165
2 strips bacon	85
coffee or tea (with/without skim milk and 1 tsp. sugar)	0-25

LUNCH
McDonald's cheeseburger   306
small french fries   211
iced tea, coffee, diet soda, water   0-25

DINNER
spaghetti squash and clams*   109
½ c. instant rice   90
½ c. raw spinach and 1 strip crumbled
    bacon (1 tbsp. diet dressing)   91
1 small strawberry shortcake   170
coffee or tea (with/without skim milk and
    1 tsp. sugar), diet soda, water   0-25

	Total	1227-1302

Day Six: Sunday

BREAKFAST
<small>Calories</small>

½ grapefruit and 1 tbsp. honey   110
1 bran muffin and 1 pat butter   140
coffee or tea (with/without skim milk and
    1 tsp. sugar)   0-25

LUNCH
1 c. crab salad on endive lettuce   155
1 c. vegetable beef soup   80
2 saltine crackers   25
3 oz. ice cream   100
iced tea, coffee, diet soda, water   0-25

DINNER
veal cutlet   185
½ baked potato with 1 pat butter or 1 tbsp.
    sour cream and chives   110
½ c. steamed winter squash with Italian
    spices   65
1 glass rosé wine   85
coffee or tea (with/without skim milk and
    1 tsp. sugar), diet soda, water   0-25

	Total	1055-1130

Day Seven: Monday

BREAKFAST   Calories
1 poached egg............................ 100
1 slice toast with 1 pat butter............ 100
6 oz. apple juice........................ 120
coffee or tea (with/without skim milk and
   1 tsp. sugar)........................ 0-25

LUNCH
fruit salad on lettuce leaf................ 126
½ c. cottage cheese..................... 200
1 blueberry muffin and 1 pat butter...... 145
iced tea, coffee, diet soda, water.......... 0-25

DINNER
1 lb. lobster with 1 tbsp. butter.......... 212
½ c. fresh steamed asparagus with
   almonds............................. 40
mixed green salad and 1 tbsp. diet
   dressing............................. 60
1 glass white wine...................... 85
coffee or tea (with/without skim milk and
   1 tsp. sugar), diet soda, water......... 0-25
                Total   1188-
                            1263

Chapter 11

Sagittarius

Sagittarius is ruled by the giant merrymaker Jupiter, the expansive planet. Your symbol, designated with an arrow, is the archer or centaur. Sagittarius rules the outdoors, philosophy, religion, and foreign lands. Sagittarians like traveling to distant lands, literally or in daydreams. You have a need for change. You're a non-conformist. You like to express your individuality. You believe that rules were meant to be broken. You don't like to be told what to do. You value freedom of expression, and you'll go to great lengths to protect that freedom. How does this affect your ability to diet? It doesn't. You are probably the least interested in dieting of all the signs of the zodiac.

Good luck always seems to follow you. It's probably your infectious optimism that attracts good fortune like a magnet. You're the friend everyone wants, because you're high-spirited and full of fun. You don't ask for a commitment from others because you hate to be tied down. Despite this, you instinctively know when your friends are in trouble and are always ready to rush to their aid.

You're always searching for a new experience. Your sense of adventure gets you into some unusual situations. Be patient with those who aren't as daring. Sagittarians seem to attract danger and excitement naturally. Sometimes you're too foolhardy for your own good. Try to look before you leap. But if you forget, don't worry, Jupiter will usually come to your rescue before any real harm is done.

Sagittarians are generous and kind. You're always loaning money to a friend or buying someone a gift for no special reason. Your generosity often leaves you short of cash, but the nice things you do for other people pay off when you're in dire straits. You have more than your share of energy. It's hard to put restrictions on a Sagittarian. You don't have a long attention span unless you're doing something that interests you. When forced to do something against your will, the happy-go-lucky Sagittarian may become moody. You are not interested in being like or unlike other people, but you only want to be yourself. You never force your ideas on anyone, and you don't want their ideas forced on you.

Your home is a fun place to visit, because you're more interested in people than you are in possessions. There's always some unusual activity going on around you. Your kitchen is the center of your home. You may use a wok or an indoor grill for most of your cooking. And the concoction on the stove might just as easily be dye for your new hobby as soup. The pâté in your Wedgwood bowl might turn out to be cat food. (Sagittarians love animals.)

You are a very gentle, kind person. Sometimes your robust personality and energy may scare other people, but usually you are in great shape. Your body craves exercise and, in many cases, your work may involve labor. Sagittarians have fewer weight problems than most of the signs in the zodiac, but more problems than the other fire signs (Aries and Leo).

Frank, a good looking, outdoorsy man, is a young executive on the rise. When he spends more time in his office than in the field, he gains weight, but he always manages to lose it at the end when he resumes his sports activities.

Sagittarians are always vowing to diet tomorrow. Since the expansive Jupiter is your ruler, you find it hard to restrict yourself by going on a diet. Jupiter natives love to experience life and all its indulgences to the fullest. Your intentions are good, but you're having such a good time that you hate to stop and start a diet. If you're overweight, it's because you love to eat. If you like to cook, try a different low carbohydrate meal every day. Include foods from other countries in your menu— stir-fry vegetables from the Orient, boiled beef dinners from Ireland, cold cuts for breakfast from Germany, or barbecue from the Southwest. If you don't like to cook, then look for quick, easy meals that can be thrown together in just a few minutes.

Exercise is the best outlet for your energy. If you really can't stand the thought of a diet, then exercise more without eating more. You're the athlete of the zodiac. Since most Sagittarians are early risers, perhaps you'd enjoy working out in the early morning. Try running or taking a brisk walk with the dog.

You enjoy the team sports like basketball, football, and rugby, but you might also like horseback riding. Or how about archery for the archer?

The charts on the following pages will help you find the best time for *you* to lose weight. The easy-to-use astrological wheel has directions on setting up your chart by using your birthday. It shows you how to follow your sun's progress through your twelve houses. The Solar Transit Chart lets you record your weight loss as the sun moves from one house to the next. There is also a first week's menu that will allow you to include the foods you and your family love in your diet.

Familiarize yourself with the astrological wheel and the significance of each house as it pertains to the Sagittarius native. The houses follow in a counterclockwise circle. Each house covers about a thirty-day period.

- When the Sagittarian sun transits your first house (Sagittarius), you want to enhance your appearance (weight loss).

- When the Sagittarian sun transits your second house (Capricorn), you want to indulge yourself (weight gain).

- When the Sagittarian sun transits your third house (Aquarius), you are better able to express your ideas.

- When the Sagittarian sun transits your fourth house (Pisces), you want to nurture yourself (weight gain).

- When the Sagittarian sun transits your fifth house (Aries), you achieve more confidence in yourself, your appearance, and your abilities (weight loss).

- When the Sagittarian sun transits your sixth house (Taurus), you become more interested in your health and working conditions.

- When the Sagittarian sun transits your seventh house (Gemini), you form new relationships and your interest in others is renewed.

- When the Sagittarian sun transits your eighth house (Cancer), you become interested in the resources of others as they affect you.

- When the Sagittarian sun transits your ninth house (Leo), you devise new plans for the future.

- When the Sagittarian sun transits your tenth house (Virgo), you move ahead with your career plans.

- When the Sagittarian sun transits your eleventh house (Libra), you want to cooperate in a group effort.

- When the Sagittarian sun transits your twelfth house

(Scorpio), you discover information previously unavailable to you.

• As the sun leaves your twelfth house and prepares to enter your first house again, you will be given a chance to reassess your last solar year and lay plans for the new year ahead.

To personalize your solar wheel insert your birthdate (month and day) in the blank space marked number 1 Sagittarius. Then, moving counterclockwise, insert the next month and same day in the blank space marked number 2 Capricorn. Continue around the solar wheel, marking the month and day in the blank spaces until you come full circle.

You will now be able to follow the sun's transits through your horoscope and anticipate what areas of your life will be highlighted each thirty-day period. The transits will also tell you the times during the year dieting will be most successful. For those people born on the cusp of a sign (three days before or three days after) refer to the Solar Position Chart to find out what your sun really is.

To see how one dieter personalized his solar wheel, see page 29.

Solar Wheel Chart

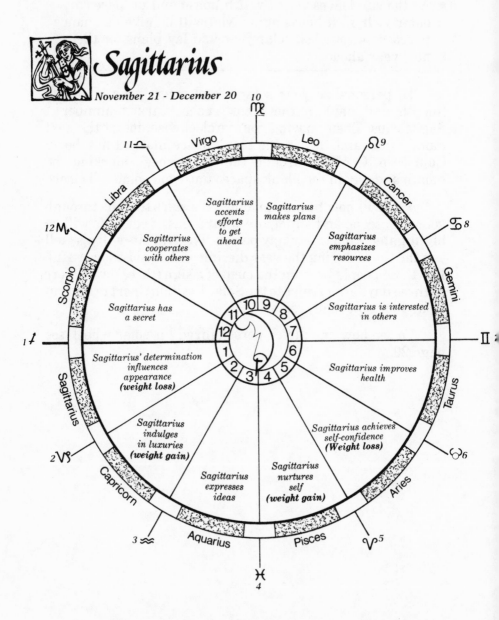

Sagittarius
November 21 - December 20

10 ♍

11 ♎   Virgo   Leo   ♌ 9

Libra   Cancer

Sagittarius accents efforts to get ahead   *Sagittarius makes plans*

12 ♏   *Sagittarius cooperates with others*   *Sagittarius emphasizes resources*   ♋ 8

Scorpio   Gemini

Sagittarius has a secret   10 9 8   *Sagittarius is interested in others*
                            11   7
1 ♐ ———   12   6 ——— ♊
                            1   5
Sagittarius' determination influences appearance (weight loss)   2 3 4   *Sagittarius improves health*

Sagittarius   Taurus

Sagittarius indulges in luxuries (weight gain)   *Sagittarius achieves self-confidence (Weight loss)*

2 ♑   *Sagittarius expresses ideas*   *Sagittarius nurtures self (weight gain)*   ♉ 6

Capricorn   Aries

3 ♒   Aquarius   Pisces   ♈ 5

♓
4

The Solar Transit Chart provides you with a guide to those times of the year when you will lose weight and those times you will gain weight.

Insert your birthdate at the top of the chart in the space marked number 1 Sagittarius. Then insert the next month and same day in the space marked number 2 Capricorn. Continue across the top of the page until you reach 12 Scorpio.

Record your total weight loss or gain with an X. At the end of the solar year, connect the Xs to reveal your astrological pattern.

To see how one dieter recorded her weight, see page 31.

Sagittarius Solar Transit Chart

House Numbers, Signs and Corresponding Dates

Lbs.	Sagittarius	Capricorn	Aquarius	Pisces	Aries	Taurus	Gemini	Cancer	Leo	Virgo	Libra	Scorpio
10												
9												
8												
7												
6												
5												
4												
3												
2												
1												
-1												
-2												
-3												
-4												
-5												
-6												
-7												
-8												
-9												
-10												

I've recommended a low carbohydrate/high protein diet, because you're a fire sign and you burn fuel efficiently. On the other hand, you probably won't like being restricted to keeping track of carbohydrates. So concentrate on the basic food groups. Be sure you get 4-7 servings of vegetables and fruits, 2-3 starches, 2 dairy products, 2 of protein, and a small amount of fats each day.

Your bones tend to be large, so you can carry more weight than most of the other signs of the zodiac without looking overweight. Don't judge by appearance alone. Check with your doctor and refer to the weight chart in Appendix A before you decide you don't need to lose weight.

Any diet will be hard, but let your sun's energy help you. You'll find it easier to diet while the sun is in your first house (November 21-December 20), and again when it enters your fifth house, Aries (March 21-April 20). When the sun enters Capricorn (around Christmas), and again when the sun enters Pisces (February 21-March 20), you may have trouble sticking with your diet. You should have less trouble as your sun progresses through Capricorn, since Saturn, its ruler, is the restricter. For best results start dieting the Thursday after a full moon.

The following is a high protein/low carbohydrate diet that incorporates the easy, but exotic dishes from all over the world you love. This diet allows you 60 grams of carbohydrates per day and all the protein you can eat. Check substitutions or exchanges with the calorie/carbohydrate/protein counter in Appendix C.

Recipes for some of the suggested dishes (marked with an asterisk) appear in Chapter 15.

Sagittarius: First Week's Menu

Day One: Thursday

BREAKFAST   Carbohydrates (in grams)
6 oz. orange juice........................ 8
hard-boiled eggs (unlimited).............. 1
piece of cheddar or hard cheese........... 1
coffee or tea (with/without heavy cream) . 0-1

LUNCH
tuna salad 3
cherry tomatoes 4
4 Ritz crackers........................... 8
1 piece of honey dew melon 11
iced tea, coffee, diet soda, water........ 0-1

DINNER
pot roast with potatoes, celery
   carrots and onions 12
salad with lettuce, tomato,
   grated cheddar cheese   6
1 glass dry red wine (claret/burgundy) ... 1
coffee or tea (with/without heavy cream) . 0-1

                                          Total   54-57

Day Two: Friday

BREAKFAST   Carbohydrates (in grams)
8 oz. V-8 juice........................... 9
1 bran muffin with butter and/or
   cream cheese 15
coffee or tea (with/without heavy cream) . 0-1

LUNCH
2 tacos or egg salad sandwich on protein
   bread 18
4 oz. of strawberries.................... 6
iced tea, coffee, diet soda, water........ 0-1

DINNER

fish cooked in butter (unlimited)	0
lettuce wedge sprinkled with grated cheese and chopped hard-boiled egg (roquefort or oil and vinegar dressing) .	4
broccoli (with butter or hollandaise sauce)	5
1 glass dry white wine (chablis, rhine)....	1
coffee or tea (with/without heavy cream) .	0-1
Total	58-61

Day Three: Saturday

BRUNCH	Carbohydrates (in grams)
1 c. cottage cheese......................	5
fresh fruit salad........................	21
1 slice protein toast with butter	9
coffee or tea (with/without heavy cream) .	0-1

DINNER

lamb chops (unlimited amount)	0
mushrooms in butter	3
spinach salad with bacon bits	5
¼ c. vanilla ice cream with one shot of creme de menthe or creme de cacao ...	14
1 glass dry red wine (claret, burgundy) ..	1
coffee or tea (with/without heavy cream) .	0-1
Total	58-60

Day Four: Sunday

BRUNCH	Carbohydrates (in grams)
8 oz. V-8 juice.........................	9
2 chicken in the basket	18
Canadian bacon (unlimited amount)......	0
coffee or tea (with/without heavy cream) .	0-1

DINNER

onion steak and mushrooms shish kebab..	4
potato salad*	12
asparagus (with butter or hollandaise sauce)	4
fresh strawberries in champagne	8
1 glass dry white wine (chablis or rhine) .	1
coffee or tea (with/without heavy cream) .	0-1
Total	56-58

Day Five: Monday

BREAKFAST Carbohydrates (in grams)

6 oz. grapefruit juice	18
1 c. Kellogg's *Special K* cereal with	7
¼ c. light cream and 1 tsp. sugar	5
coffee or tea (with/without heavy cream) .	0-1

LUNCH

beef noodle soup	5
chicken salad	2
iced tea, coffee, diet soda, water	0-1

DINNER

martini or scotch on the rocks	1
Mexican chicken*	9
piece of cheddar cheese	1
avocado, lettuce & tomato salad (use salad dressing sparingly)	5
coffee or tea (with/without heavy cream) .	0-1
Total	53-56

Day Six: Tuesday

BREAKFAST Carbohydrates (in grams)

Canadian bacon	0
1 slice of protein toast with butter	9
8 oz. V-8 juice	9
coffee or tea (with/without heavy cream) .	0-1

LUNCH

hamburger patty (unlimited amount)	0
hard-boiled eggs	1
iced tea, coffee, diet soda, water	0-1

DINNER

stir-fried chicken, cauliflower and carrots	11
½ c. rice	21
4 oz. raw papaya	7
coffee or tea (with/without heavy cream) .	0-1
Total	58-61

Day Seven: Wednesday

BREAKFAST	Carbohydrates (in grams)
orange breakfast drink	29
coffee or tea (with/without heavy cream) .	0-1

LUNCH	
chicken bouillon........................	0
tuna salad with vegetables*	6
iced tea, coffee, diet soda, water..........	0-1

DINNER	
meat loaf with no filler (unlimited amount)	0
boiled potatoes	12
green beans in butter with slivered almonds	6
1 glass dry red wine (claret, burgundy) ..	1
coffee or tea (with/without heavy cream) .	0-1
Total	**54-57**

Chapter 12

Capricorn

Capricorn's ruling planet is the taskmaster, Saturn. Capricorn is symbolized by the sure-footed mountain goat who is always aspiring to higher and higher places. Your sign represents public recognition, honors, career, and authority. If any sign in the zodiac is disciplined, it's you. The Capricorn child seems wiser and more mature than his or her sister signs.

Things do not come easy to you, but you've learned that what's worth having is worth waiting for. Along with Virgo, you're the most practical sign in the zodiac. Chance never enters into your scheme of things. You achieve your goals. But, like the mountain goat, you're always looking up at the ledge. You're a hard worker. You don't let the magnitude of the job overwhelm you. You take one step at a time, never allowing any obstacle to stand in your way. You shoulder many responsibilities. You are loyal, trustworthy and dependable.

Your career is one of the most important things in your life. You have a lot to contribute. You more than justify your existence each and every day. You prefer to keep a low profile.

You like to work behind the scenes. You can and do organize anything (many of our presidents were Capricorns).

You're the most honorable of the signs. You always try to keep your word, and you'd never ask anyone to do anything you wouldn't do yourself. Some see you as a hard taskmaster because of that. You like the proven ways of doing things. You like anything that reminds you of the past. You collect antiques because they're made better, they're a good investment, and they've stood the test of time. The past gives you the sense of a solid foundation on which to build your life.

You're a rather formal person, and you tend to let your head rule your heart. You'd never think of jumping into a relationship without first taking a long, hard look at the situation. Once you're involved in a relationship, you're one of the most faithful lovers or one of the truest friends. Serious by nature, you seldom allow yourself the luxury of communicating your feelings to others. It then stands to reason that you are sometimes misunderstood. Underneath your stolid exterior, you're sensitive. You'd love to have a close, sharing relationship with someone who'd respect and appreciate you. All in all, you are the most misunderstood sign in the zodiac. It's all very well to be singleminded, but don't let life pass you by. Slow down and smell the flowers and feel the sunshine.

Fantasy has no place in your world. You're the doubting Thomas of the zodiac. Capricorns take nothing on faith. You're always struggling to gain control of your destiny. There are those who want to dominate you, but you'll rise above them to become your own boss. Even as a child, you had to struggle against this kind of oppression and you were labeled stubborn by your parents and teachers.

There appears to be a cosmic bond between Capricorn and Cancer natives. As cardinal signs, you are both initiators and self-protectors at the same time. Where Cancer retreats to his or her shell when threatened, the Capricorn native surrounds him or herself with a cloak of superiority and bravado. In reality you're a very shy person trying to do the best job you know how. You are good at whatever you are interested in and you know it. You have every right to be confident in your ability.

Appearances are very important to you. You're always trying to impress others. As soon as you can, you'll own a home in the best part of town, drive a nice car, and dress appropriately for every occasion. You do everything the hard way— alone. But you seem to like it that way. You will enjoy a long life because you're basically a healthy person. You've learned the importance of a healthy body and you take care of yourself. Capricorns usually have medium to large frames. You usually won't deal with weight problems until you're over thirty and well on your way to reaching your goals. After thirty, you begin to realize hard work isn't the important thing in life. In order to be at your best, you realize you must look your best.

Take Glen, for example. He's a very distinguished-looking gentleman in his early forties. On his last birthday, he decided to go on an all-out self-improvement program. Like most Capricorns, he researched his desirable weight and then decided on the best course of action. He has lost thirty-three pounds, you'll find him running a mile or two every morning.

Dick also decided to diet right after his thirty-seventh birthday, but he claims astrology had nothing to do with it. His parting words on the subject were, "Well, what do you expect? I'm a Capricorn and we are not supposed to believe."

If you think you're overweight check the weight chart in Appendix A and double check with your doctor. If you and your doctor determine you're consuming far too many calories, try cutting down on business lunches. Ambitious Capricorns should order the diet platter instead of the daily special.

When eating alone, you're frugal. When entertaining others, you will only serve the best. You're a conservative cook. You like to stick with old favorites; you don't often venture into new cuisine. Because you work hard, you may skip meals and eat junk food on the run. You probably need more fiber or roughage in your diet to help stimulate digestion. Fiber is low in calories, high in water content and, therefore, filling. It may even decrease your chances of developing certain types of cancer. You probably don't get enough Vitamin C either. One doctor has found that Vitamin C may, in addition to preventing colds, help burn up calories.

Saturn's Day (Saturday) after the full moon is the day to begin your diet. Earth signs don't usually binge. Instead their weight gain in usually gradual. You can't help but be interested in dieting around your birthday or when your sun enters Taurus (April 21-May 20). You will just naturally take steps to improve your self-image by going on a strict, disciplined program.

When your Capricorn sun enters Aquarius, your second house (January 21-February 20), you may want to reward yourself for losing weight. Go ahead, but don't reward yourself with food. When the sun enters your fourth house, Aries (March 21-April 20), you may find your weight loss will slacken. Stick to your diet during this time. Don't get discouraged. You have the rest of the year to stick to your routine and reach your goal.

Think seriously about learning golf or tennis. Bicycling and jogging offer another exercise alternative. First, These activities have the advantage of providing a cheap mode of transportation, a chance to slow down and enjoy the scenery, and it gives you time alone to make your plans.

People born under a Capricorn sun never seem to get older. They only seem to get better, and that applies to you.

The charts on the following pages will help you find the best time for *you* to lose weight. The easy-to-use astrological wheel has directions on setting up your chart by using your birthday. It shows you how to follow your sun's progress through your twelve houses. The Solar Transit Chart lets you record your weight loss as the sun moves from one house to the next. There is also a first week's menu that will allow you to include the foods you and your family love in your diet.

Familiarize yourself with the astrological wheel and the significance of each house as it pertains to the Capricorn native. The houses follow in a counterclockwise circle. Each house covers about a thirty-day period.

- When the Capricorn sun transits your first house (Capricorn), you want to enhance your appearance (weight loss).

- When the Capricorn sun transits your second house (Aquarius), you wnat to indulge yourself (weight gain).

- When the Capricorn sun transits your third house (Pisces), you are better able to express your ideas.

- When the Capricorn sun transits your fourth house (Aries), you want to nurture yourself (weight gain).

- When the Capricorn sun transits your fifth house (Taurus), you achieve more confidence in yourself, your appearance, and your abilities (weight loss).

- When the Capricorn sun transits your sixth house (Gemini), you become more interested in your health and working conditions.

- When the Capricorn sun transits your seventh house (Cancer), you form new relationships and your interest in others is renewed.

- When the Capricorn sun transits your eighth house (Leo), you become interested in the resources of others as they affect you.

- When the Capricorn sun transits your ninth house (Virgo), you devise new plans for the future.

- When the Capricorn sun transits your tenth house (Libra), you move ahead with your career plans.

- When the Capricorn sun transits your eleventh house (Scorpio), you want to cooperate in a group effort.

- When the Capricorn sun transits your twelfth house (Sagittarius), you discover information previously unavailable to you.

- As the sun leaves your twelfth house and prepares to enter your first house again, you will be given a chance to reassess your last solar year and lay plans for the new year ahead.

To personalize your solar wheel insert your birthdate (month and day) in the blank space marked number 1 Capricorn. Then, moving counterclockwise, insert the next month and same day in the blank space marked number 2 Aquarius. Continue around the solar wheel marking the month and day in the blank spaces until you come full circle.

You will now be able to follow the sun's transits through your horoscope and anticipate what areas of your life will be highlighted each thirty-day period. The transits will also tell you the times during the year dieting will be most successful. For those people born on the cusp of a sign (three days before or three days after) refer to the Solar Position Chart to find out what your sun really is.

To see how one dieter personalized his solar wheel, see page 29.

Solar Wheel Chart

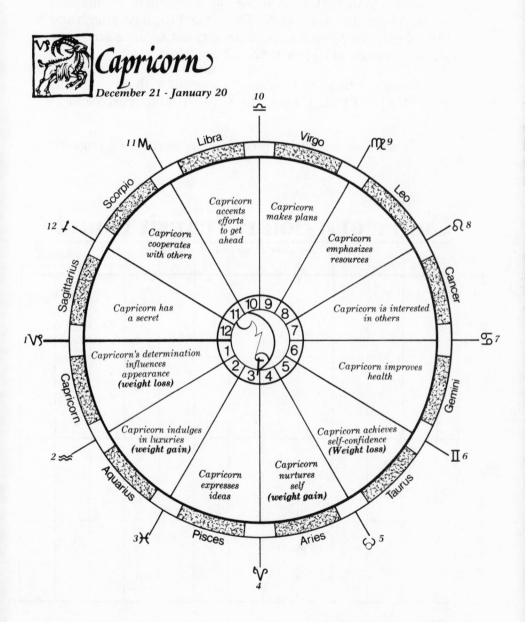

Capricorn

December 21 - January 20

Capricorn accents efforts to get ahead

Capricorn makes plans

Capricorn cooperates with others

Capricorn emphasizes resources

Capricorn has a secret

Capricorn is interested in others

Capricorn's determination influences appearance *(weight loss)*

Capricorn improves health

Capricorn indulges in luxuries *(weight gain)*

Capricorn achieves self-confidence *(Weight loss)*

Capricorn expresses ideas

Capricorn nurtures self *(weight gain)*

Libra — Virgo — Scorpio — Leo — Sagittarius — Cancer — Capricorn — Gemini — Aquarius — Taurus — Pisces — Aries

The Solar Transit Chart provides you with a guide to those times of the year when you will lose weight and those times you will gain weight.

Insert your birthdate at the top of the chart in the space marked number 1 Capricorn. Then insert the next month and same day in the space marked 2 Aquarius. Continue across the top of the page until you reach 12 Sagittarius.

Record your total weight loss or gain with an X. At the end of the solar year, connect the Xs to reveal your astrological pattern.

To see how one dieter recorded her weight, see page 31.

Capricorn Solar Transit Chart

	House Numbers, Signs and Corresponding Dates											
Lbs.	Capricorn	Aquarius	Pisces	Aries	Taurus	Gemini	Cancer	Leo	Virgo	Libra	Scorpio	Sagittarius
10												
9												
8												
7												
6												
5												
4												
3												
2												
1												
-1												
-2												
-3												
-4												
-5												
-6												
-7												
-8												
-9												
-10												

The diet plan I outlined is low in calories. Allow yourself 1200 calories a day if you're a woman, 1500 calories a day if you're a man. Check substitutions and exchanges in the calorie/carbohydrate/protein counter provided in Appendix C. When you reach your goal, gradually increase your calorie intake until you find the level that will let you maintain your weight. Consult your doctor before starting this or any other diet. Recipes for some of the suggested dishes (marked with an asterisk) can be found in Chapter 15.

Capricorn: First Week's Menu

Day One: Saturday

BREAKFAST	Calories
1 c. vegetable juice	40
1 vegetable omelette.....................	260-360
1 cup coffee or tea (with/without skim milk and 1 tsp. sugar).................	0-25

LUNCH	
4 oz. steamed shrimp on lettuce	108
1 cup Manhattan clam chowder	81
1 apple	61
1 cup coffee or tea (with/without skim milk and 1 tsp. sugar), diet soda, water	0-25

DINNER	
½ 10″ cheese pizza......................	500
salad with 1 tbsp. diet dressing	60
1 glass light beer, diet soda, water	0-80
Total	1110-1340

Day Two: Sunday

BREAKFAST	Calories
1 serving Eggs Benedict.................	296
fruit salad	126
1 cup coffee or tea (with/without skim milk and 1 tsp. sugar).................	0-25

LUNCH

1 lb. lobster with 1 tbsp. butter	212
4 oz. steak	235
½ baked potato with 1 pat butter (or 1 tbsp. sour cream and chives)...............	111
salad with 1 tbsp. diet dressing	60
1 glass wine, diet soda, water	0-90
1 cup coffee or tea (with/without skim milk and 1 tsp. sugar).................	0-25

DINNER

1 open-face melted cheese sandwich with tomato	185
½ c. tomato soup	55
1 cup coffee or tea (with/without skim milk and 1 tsp. sugar), diet soda, water	0-25
Total	1280-1445

Day Three: Monday

BREAKFAST
Calories

½ small cantaloupe	58
1 slice toast with 1 pat butter	106
1 cup coffee or tea (with/without skim milk and 1 tsp. sugar).................	0-25

LUNCH

egg salad sandwich with 1 tbsp. mayonnaise and lettuce leaf	310
celery sticks	10
carrot sticks	21
1 small cookie..........................	50
1 cup coffee or tea (with/without skim milk and 1 tsp. sugar), diet soda, water	0-25

DINNER

onions, steak, and mushrooms*..........	330
lettuce wedge with 1 tbsp. diet dressing ..	40
½ c. zucchini	55
1 glass chianti, diet soda, water	0-100
dessert (your choice)....................	226
Total	1206-1356

Day Four: Tuesday

BREAKFAST   Calories

1 c. unsweetened grapefruit juice	101
1 c. *Kellogg's Special K* cereal (½ c. skim milk and 1 tsp. sugar).................	0-25

LUNCH

McDonald's cheeseburger................	306
small french fries	211
1 cup coffee or tea (with/without skim milk and 1 tsp. sugar), diet soda, water	0-25

DINNER

8 oz. flounder	180
½ c. cole slaw	60
½ c. steamed carrots and 1 pat butter and herbs	59
½ cantaloupe	58
1 cup coffee or tea (with/without skim milk and 1 tsp. sugar), diet soda, water	0-25
Total	1104-1179

Day Five: Wednesday

BREAKFAST   Calories

½ papaya	60
1 piece french toast (1 tsp. maple syrup)..	175
1 cup coffee or tea (with/without skim milk and 1 tsp. sugar).................	0-25

LUNCH

1 cup chicken noodle soup	65
chef salad (lettuce, tomato, 1 slice cheese, 1 oz. ham, 1 hard boiled egg, and 1 tbsp. diet dressing)	315
1 cup coffee or tea (with/without skim milk and 1 tsp. sugar), diet soda, water	0-25

DINNER

spinach salad*	160
4 oz. chicken	200
½ c. instant rice	71

½ c. yellow squash steamed with
1 pat butter   50
mock melba...........................   88
1 cup coffee or tea (with/without skim milk
and 1 tsp. sugar), diet soda, water 0-25

                              Total   1184-
                                       1259

Day Six: Thursday

BREAKFAST Calories
½ grapefruit with ½ tbsp. honey..........   85
1 c. puffed wheat or puffed rice (½ c. skim
milk and 1 tsp. sugar)................. 110
1 cup coffee or tea (with/without skim
milk and 1 tsp. sugar)................. 0-25

LUNCH
⅓ c. cottage cheese with ½ c. fresh fruit
on lettuce leaf 110
blueberry muffin and 1 pat butter 176
1 cup coffee or tea (with/without skim milk
and 1 tsp. sugar), diet soda, water 0-25

DINNER
beef and tomato and pepper kabobs 260
double-baked potato* 100
½ c. broccoli steamed with herbs   20
2 small cookies 100
1 cup coffee or tea (with/without skim milk
and 1 tsp. sugar), diet soda, water 0-25

                              Total   961-
                                       1036

Day Seven: Friday

BREAKFAST Calories
1 c. orange juice....................... 120
1 egg cooked any way 100
1 slice toast with 1 pat of butter.......... 106
1 cup coffee or tea (with/without skim
milk and 1 tsp. sugar)................. 0-25

LUNCH

½ c. tuna salad on 280
    lettuce leaf 5
1 dill pickle 10
1 cup coffee or tea (with/without skim milk
    and 1 tsp. sugar), diet soda, water 0-25

DINNER

beef stew 240
lettuce and tomato salad (1 tbsp. diet
    dressing) 60
dessert peaches......................... 50
1 glass lite beer 80
1 cup coffee or tea (with/without skim milk
    and 1 tsp. sugar), diet soda, water 0-25

                      Total   1051-
                                 1126

Chapter 13

Aquarius

Though Aquarius is an air sign, it's symbol is the water bearer. Your sun sign rules friendships, organizations, hopes and wishes, and humanity. Uranus, your ruling planet, is volatile. Aquarians are inventors, reformers, rebels, and humanitarians. You're interested in progress, and might be considered a non-conformist. People enjoy being with you. No one knows quite what to expect from you. You're full of surprises, so when it comes to dieting, it's much easier for you to break away from old, destructive eating habits than for any of the other signs in the zodiac.

You want to better the human condition: whether it's on the picket lines, at the polls, or in a schoolroom, you can be counted on to do more than your share of the work. For you a job has to be enjoyable and useful, or you won't do it. You're always working for the common good, and you have little interest in material goods. You have the capacity to do great things, and you live up to your capacity. You hold out hope for the rest of us.

As the individualist of the zodiac, you're definitely not one of the crowd. Instead, you're uniquely you. Since you're the last fixed sign, you're the proverbial "a friend indeed."

You present a detached, cool face to the world. You approach life with the pragmatism of a scientist studying the results of his or her experiment. Emotions don't usually enter into it.

Like the Sagittarian native, you want the freedom to pursue your interests. You seldom get emotionally involved in a relationship until later in life, after you've done what you set out to do. With the volatile Uranus as your ruling planet, you can change character before people's eyes. Uranus brings you in contact with unusual people and situations. Tagging along with you can be exciting for the rest of us.

You know how to express yourself in an original way, but you don't mind sharing the spotlight. You're the original trendsetter. You have excellent taste in clothes; you always seem to be one step ahead of the designers. Aquarians are often found in the scientific and technological professions. You usually put your work ahead of your feelings.

You look for the similarities between people. As a child, you tried to find out how other people were like you, and you hated to fight over differences of any kind. Your ability to see the similarities in people enables you to organize people into a team and supply them with a common goal. There is nothing mean, petty, or possessive about you. You're interested in relationships, and you'll go to great lengths to try to forestall a confrontation. You'd rather talk than fight. You respect other's rights to their own opinions, but you won't compromise your own integrity. You're someone with strong likes and dislikes. But this does not include material possessions. This is not to say that you don't like your comforts and conveniences— because you do—but going after material possessions as an end in itself turns you off. You want to do right by the world and humanity and you are willing to sacrifice a lot, but you really do hate to give up your comfort. Cheer up, even though you lack an interest in material things, they still seem to come to you in mysterious, unusual ways and are usually one-of-a-kind and are of the very best quality. The rest of us wish we were so lucky!

If you're interested in a project, you may forget to eat. You'd hate to stop in the middle of something just to eat. Consequently, you have less of a weight problem than most of the other signs. Carolyn, a nurse who is an unpredictable Aquarian, doesn't think dieting is important. She's pretty, well-traveled, and adventurous. I asked her when and how she lost weight. She replied that whenever her clothes get a little tight, she just loses. Oh that it were as simple for the rest of us.

If an Aquarian is overweight, they're often unaware of the problem until someone voices their concern. Ironically, you may counsel and encourage other people to lose weight while being overweight yourself. We're likely to find you volunteering for a hunger relief committee. You're too thoughtful and unselfish and too worried about the fate of others to be concerned about yourself. Even if you weigh a few pounds too many, you're certainly doing your part to make the world a nicer place.

If you've checked the Desirable Weight Chart in Appendix A and decided you're overweight consult your doctor to be sure that your weight gain isn't the result of some medical problem. If overeating is the problem, it's probably because you don't pay enough attention to what you are eating. Too often, you eat what's handy instead of what's most nutritious. Try to pay attention to what you are eating. Snacking isn't bad as long as you eat foods that are lower in calories than your usual fare. Try raw vegetables and dried, fresh or frozen fruits. Channel some of your creative energy into thinking up ways to cut calories and improve your diet. Start a low-calorie gourmet club; share your diet innovations with overweight friends and colleagues. Your enthusiasm will inspire everyone, including you.

You have welcomed weary travelers from all over the world. Your home is where people gather to meet and exchange ideas because you know how to make them feel comfortable and relaxed. Your home is filled with energy-saving devices. Your kitchen, one of the most important rooms of the house, probably has a microwave oven and a home computer. There may be solar panels on the roof, or a windmill on the hill. Your home may be chaotic, especially at mealtime. Because of the unpredictable nature of your life, odd things just charge in and carry you away so that meals are served at any time, and can consist of anything—hot dogs one night, Beef Wellington the next. As for any children you might have, life with you is an Auntie Mame experience—as she says in the movie, "Life is a banquet with so much to sample, and most poor suckers are starving to death." "Live, live, live!"

Many of your friends are not as adventuresome, or as creative as you, so you are always trying new foods and techniques out on them. Maybe you can start a low-calorie gourmet club with others in your neighborhood who share the same problem of being overweight. Begin to guide and support them in their endeavor to lose weight and everyone will benefit, especially you.

Because Aquarius is a fixed sign, weight you gain is harder to lose. Most Aquarians maintain a constant weight that rarely fluctuates. If you do feel the need to lose weight, you'll usually have to change your eating habits drastically. You should consider engaging in new daily exercise. Your ruling planet, Uranus, demands radical changes in your life from time to time. Besides, it could be fun to do something different.

The times when you are most likely to gain are when the sun transits your second house, Pisces (February 21-March 20), and again when your sun enters Taurus (April 21-May 20). But when the sun moves into Gemini (May 21-June 20), the weight you've gained should come right off. Your most dramatic weight loss appears to coincide with your birthday. Your appetite should decrease and you'll become involved in some new project around that time. A diet started on your birthday should require little effort on your part. Your diet will bring the best results if you begin on a Saturday after the full moon.

Though Aquarians often look delicate, you're basically healthy. Most Aquarians don't like exercise; any form of discipline goes over like a wet blanket with you. But exercise doesn't have to be rigid. Organize a co-ed baseball team, soccer team, or a relay race to raise money for a worthy cause. You'll probably look great in a team uniform.

The charts on the following pages will help you find the best time for *you* to lose weight. The easy-to-use astrological wheel has directions on setting up your chart by using your birthday. It shows you how to follow your sun's progress through your twelve houses. The Solar Transit Chart lets you record your weight loss as the sun moves from one house to the next. There is also a first week's menu that will allow you to include the foods you and your family love in your diet.

Familiarize yourself with the astrological wheel and the significance of each house as it pertains to the Aquarius native. The houses follow in a counterclockwise circle. Each house covers about a thirty day period.

- When the Aquarius sun transits your first house (Aquarius), you want to enhance your appearance (weight loss).

- When the Aquarius sun transits your second house (Pisces), you want to indulge yourself (weight gain).

- When the Aquarius sun transits your third house (Aries), you are better able to express your ideas.

- When the Aquarius sun transits your fourth house (Taurus), you want to nurture yourself (weight gain).

- When the Aquarius sun transits your fifth house (Gemini), you achieve more confidence in yourself, your appearance, and your abilities (weight loss).

- When the Aquarius sun transits your sixth house

(Cancer), you become more interested in your health and working conditions.

- When the Aquarius sun transits your seventh house (Leo), you form new relationships and your interest in others is renewed.

- When the Aquarius sun transits your eighth house (Virgo), you become interested in the resources of others as they affect you.

- When the Aquarius sun transits your ninth house (Libra), you devise new plans for the future.

- When the Aquarius sun transits your tenth house (Scorpio), you move ahead with your career plans.

- When the Aquarius sun transits your eleventh house (Sagittarius), you want to cooperate in a group effort.

- When the Aquarius sun transits your twelfth house (Capricorn), you discover information previously unavailable to you.

- As the sun leaves your twelfth house and prepares to enter your first house again, you will be given a chance to reassess your last solar year and lay plans for the new year ahead.

To personalize your solar wheel insert your birthdate (month and day) in the blank space marked number 1 Aquarius. Then, moving counterclockwise, insert the next month and same day in the blank space marked number 2 Pisces. Continue around the solar wheel marking the month and day in the blank spaces until you come full circle.

You will now be able to follow the sun's transits through your horoscope and anticipate what areas of your life will be highlighted each thirty-day period. The transits will also tell you the times during the year dieting will be most successful. For those people born on the cusp of a sign (three days before or three days after) refer to the Solar Position Chart to find out what your sun really is.

Solar Wheel Chart

To see how one dieter personalized his solar wheel, see page 29.

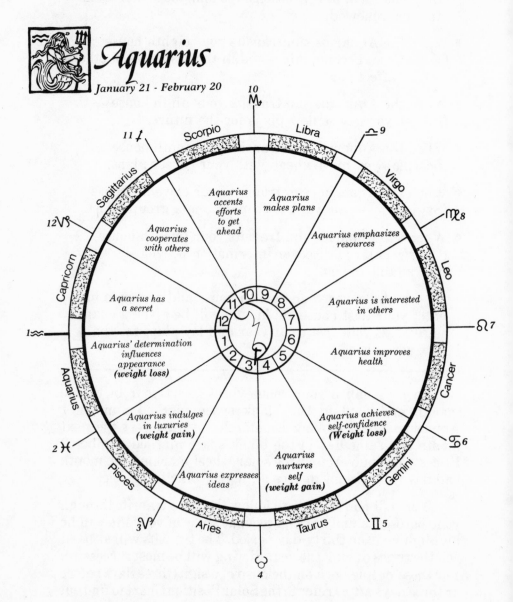

Aquarius

January 21 - February 20

- 10 ♏
- 11 ♐
- Scorpio
- Libra
- 9 ♎
- Sagittarius
- Virgo
- 12 ♑
- ♍ 8
- Capricorn
- Leo
- 1 ♒
- ♌ 7
- Aquarius
- Cancer
- 2 ♓
- ♋ 6
- Pisces
- Gemini
- 3 ♈
- Aries
- Taurus
- ♊ 5
- ♉ 4

Aquarius accents efforts to get ahead

Aquarius makes plans

Aquarius cooperates with others

Aquarius emphasizes resources

Aquarius has a secret

Aquarius is interested in others

Aquarius' determination influences appearance (weight loss)

Aquarius improves health

Aquarius indulges in luxuries (weight gain)

Aquarius achieves self-confidence (Weight loss)

Aquarius expresses ideas

Aquarius nurtures self (weight gain)

The Solar Transit Chart provides you with a guide to those times of the year when you will lose weight and those times you will gain weight.

Insert your birthdate at the top of the chart in the space marked number 1 Aquarius. Then insert the next month and same day in the space marked number 2 Pisces. Continue across the top of the page until you reach number 12 Capricorn.

Record your total weight loss or gain with an X. At the end of the solar year, connect the Xs to reveal your astrological pattern.

To see how one dieter recorded her weight, see page 31.

Aquarius Solar Transit Chart

House Numbers, Signs and Corresponding Dates

Lbs.	Aquarius	Pisces	Aries	Taurus	Gemini	Cancer	Leo	Virgo	Libra	Scorpio	Sagittarius	Capricorn
10												
9												
8												
7												
6												
5												
4												
3												
2												
1												
-1												
-2												
-3												
-4												
-5												
-6												
-7												
-8												
-9												
-10												

The diet outlined below is low in calories and incorporates many unusual, easy-to-prepare dishes. You are allowed 1200 calories a day if you're a woman, 1500 calories a day if you're a man. Check substitutions and exchanges with the calorie/carbohydrate/protein counter found in Appendix C. To take best advantage of the recommended diet plan, eat your meals in a relaxed, congenial setting. Recipes for some of the suggested dishes (marked with an asterisk) appear in Chapter 15.

Aquarius: First Week's Menu

Day One: Saturday

BREAKFAST	Calories
1 egg cooked any way	100
1 cup coffee or tea (with/without skim milk and 1 tsp. sugar)................	0-25
SNACK	
1 small apple...........................	80
4 oz. orange juice......................	60
LUNCH	
chef salad (lettuce, tomato, 1 slice cheese, 1 oz. ham, 1 hard-boiled egg, and 1 tbsp. diet dressing).........................	315
diet soda, mineral water, water	0-25
SNACK	
1 bran muffin and 1 pat butter	136
1 cup coffee or tea (with/without skim milk and 1 tsp. sugar)................	0-25
DINNER	
shrimp and snow peas*	200
½ c. instant rice	71
½ c. steamed carrots and herbs	20
iced herbal tea, mineral water, water	0-25
SNACK	
2 small fig cookies......................	100
6 oz. lite cocoa	70
Total	1152-1252

Day Two: Sunday

BREAKFAST Calories

1 c. puffed wheat or puffed rice (½ c.
skim milk and 1 tsp. sugar) 110
1 cup coffee or tea (with/without skim
milk and 1 tsp. sugar)................. 0-25

SNACK

Hawaiian breakfast drink* 96

LUNCH

open-face melted cheese sandwich
with tomato 185
celery sticks 10
carrot sticks 21
diet soda, mineral water, water 0-25

SNACK

¼ cantaloupe 30
6 oz. apple cider....................... 90

DINNER

4 oz. lamb chop 140
½ c. broccoli and herbs 20
½ baked yam with 1 pat butter 116
iced herbal tea, mineral water, water 0-25

SNACK

¼ c. unshelled pumpkin seeds 60
2 c. lightly salted popcorn 100
6 oz. apple cider....................... 90

Total   1068-
1143

Day Three: Monday

BREAKFAST Calories

1 c. oatmeal (with ½ c. skim milk
and 1 tsp. sugar)..................... 195
coffee or tea (with/without skim
milk and 1 tsp. sugar)................. 0-25

SNACK

orange breakfast drink* 200

LUNCH
2 tacos.................................... 360
diet soda, mineral water, water 0-25

SNACK
½ c. yogurt with ½ c. strawberries........ 65
herbal tea............................... 0

DINNER
egg omelette with mushrooms and 1 slice
   cooked bacon 270
lettuce and tomato salad with 1 tbsp.
   diet dressing.......................... 60
iced herbal tea, mineral water, water 0-25

SNACK
1 c. chicken bouillon..................... 20
2 saltine crackers 25

Total   1195-
                   1270

Day Four: Tuesday

BREAKFAST
Calories
½ cantaloupe 60
1 cup coffee or tea (with/without skim
   milk and 1 tsp. sugar)................. 0-25

SNACK
4 oz. orange juice....................... 60
corn muffin and 1 pat butter 166

LUNCH
4 oz. shrimp salad 210
1 c. chicken and rice soup............... 45
diet soda, mineral water, water 0-25

SNACK
carrot, zucchini and cucumber chips 41
4 oz. vegetable juice 20

DINNER
stewed chicken.......................... 200
lettuce and tomato salad with 1 tbsp.
   diet dressing.......................... 60
iced herbal tea, mineral water, water 0-25

SNACK
½ apple	35
grapes	50
1 oz. swiss cheese	105
herbal tea	0-25
Total	1052-1152

Day Five: Wednesday

BREAKFAST Calories
6 oz. grapefruit juice	75
1 slice french toast (1 tsp. maple syrup)	175
1 cup coffee or tea (with/without skim milk and 1 tsp. sugar)	0-25

SNACK
½ c. fresh strawberries	20
8 oz. skim milk	90

LUNCH
½ c. plain cottage cheese with tomato on lettuce leaf	130
1 hard-boiled egg	82
diet soda, mineral water, water	0-25

SNACK
1 oz. cheese and 4 saltine crackers	160
1 glass dry wine	85

DINNER
4 oz. broiled filet sole	80
4 stalks asparagus with herb or lemon juice	10
spaghetti squash with 1 pat butter	100
iced herbal tea, mineral water, water	0-25

SNACK
baked apple	130
herbal tea	0-25
Total	1137-1237

Day Six: Thursday

BREAKFAST   Calories
1 blueberry muffin with 1 pat butter 176
coffee or tea (with/without skim milk
    and 1 tsp. sugar) 0-25

SNACK
4 oz. orange juice   60
fruit salad 126

LUNCH
3½ oz. shrimp with cocktail sauce 125
½ c. Manhattan clam chowder   35
diet soda, mineral water, water 0-25

SNACK
stuffed celery sticks   40
carrot sticks   21
radishes   5
4 oz. vegetable juice   20

DINNER
4 oz. steak 235
½ baked potato with 1 pat butter or 1 tbsp.
    sour cream and chives 111
lettuce and tomato salad with 1 tbsp.
    diet dressing........................   60
iced herbal tea, mineral water, water 0-25

SNACK
strawberry shortcake 140
decaffeinated coffee or herbal tea (with/
    without skim milk and 1 tsp. sugar) ... 0-25

                              Total   1154-
                                         1254

Day Seven: Friday

BREAKFAST   Calories
½ fresh-squeezed lemon in 1 cup hot water
   with 1 tsp. honey...................... 35
1 slice whole wheat toast and 1 pat butter   101
1 cup coffee or tea (with/without skim
   milk and 1 tsp. sugar)................ 0-25

SNACK
5 dried apricots or 3 fresh apricots....... 55
4 oz. skim milk.......................... 45

LUNCH
McDonald's cheeseburger................ 306
diet soda, mineral water, water.......... 0-25

SNACK
zucchini and cucumber chips............ 20
cherry tomatoes........................ 20
herbal tea.............................. 0-25

DINNER
½ 10″ cheese pizza...................... 500
salad and 1 tbsp. diet dressing........... 60
iced herbal tea, mineral water, water 0-25

SNACK
pineapple yogurt shake 135
                         Total   1277-
                                       1377

Chapter 14

Pisces

P isces, you're the twelfth and last house in the zodiac. Your sign represents secrets, the unconscious, imagination, mystery, intuition, dreams, and all things hidden. Neptune is your ruling planet, and your symbol is the elusive fish. You govern water in its gaseous state (steam). You are benevolent and tenderhearted. Pisces is the protector of sailors, actors, prophets, and mystics. You are the great counselor. Its natives possess ideals, inspiration, vision, and imagination. You're the mystic of the zodiac. You seem to have a sixth sense.

Pisceans are quiet, dreamy, unpretentious people. Your friends and family are protective of you because of your gentleness. But you don't really need protection because your sixth sense keeps you out of harm's way. You're sensitive to the people around you and you can change your mood to suit the situation. Your acute awareness of others can be draining, because when those you care about are unhappy or depressed, you become unhappy and depressed, too.

You cry more easily than any other sign in the zodiac. It's hard for other people to understand how deeply you care and

174

how much you identify with others, be they people, plants, or animals. Because you're so easily hurt, you've created an inner haven, your private garden, where you can retreat when life overwhelms you. But, more often than not, you don't need to retreat, for Pisceans tend to see the world through rose-colored glasses, and you can convince the rest of us to believe in your vision. Your rose-colored glasses help you recognize the true potential of others. Your insight and advice enables them to realize that potential.

You were probably an excellent student. As a child, you were anxious to please; you always tried to do the right thing. If you didn't live up to your parents' expectations, you felt guilty, even if you'd done nothing wrong. It was and is hard for you to accept that there are things in life you have no control over. Pisces natives hate violence. You'll usually avoid any sport or kind of exercise where someone might get hurt. You even dislike angry words. Instead, you prefer music, writing, painting, sculpting or reading. Pisces natives are avid writers and readers. Many Pisceans make writing their profession.

When you shy Pisces natives reveal yourselves, people realize you're not aloof. Old-fashioned bashfulness is one of the lovable qualities about a Piscean. You never enter into a relationship lightly, because you're afraid you might be hurt. But when you do decide to open up, there's nothing shy or timid about you. You're one of the most generous, sympathetic, loving people in the zodiac. You give yourself freely and expect nothing in return. But you will be rewarded for all your kindness.

It may be hard for you to believe, but you are really very good at a lot of different things. You are wonderfully creative. Many people envy your child-like innocence which enables you to see the beauty in everything around you and interpret it.

Home is where you love to be. There are many wonderful, artistic touches that make it interesting. Pictures in vibrant colors line the walls, and there may be a sculpture here and there. Most of the artwork is by you, your spouse, friends, relatives, or children. Pisceans have a knack for interior decorating, and they love creating an attractive, inviting atmosphere.

A Pisces kitchen is like a surprise party. You'll try any recipe once. But take care, Pisceans are prone to food allergies. Pisceans can also become addicted to foods such as coffee, coca cola, or chocolate and undetected allergies or addiction to certain foods could be the key to any excessive weight gain. You love to cook, but you don't do it by the book. You never put things together the same way twice. A pinch of this, a dash of that, and you're done—a dish fit for a king (or queen).

Your weight problems are cyclic: you go through fat and thin phases. You don't usually overeat much, but you feel as guilty as if you did. Your guilt feelings may cause you to overeat even more, gain weight, and feel even more guilty than before. Stop that vicious cycle now. Don't you know you're beautiful the way you look right now, even if you are a little overweight? Pisceans rule things that are hidden, and you hide the best part of you from yourself.

Your weight can fluctuate up to five or ten pounds because you retain a lot of fluid. A change in eating habits and a decrease in your salt intake starting after a full moon will alleviate your water weight problem. Check with your doctor to be sure your weight gain isn't due to a medical problem, and never start this or any other diet without his or her approval. Plan your diet strategy with a supportive friend. Don't worry if you go off your diet occasionally. There'll be times when you'll find it almost impossible to stay on your diet because of your horoscope. When the sun transits your fourth house and the sign, Gemini (May 21-June 20), and again when the sun crosses into Aries (March 21-April 20), you'll find dieting difficult. But when the sun is in Aries, you'll have little problem maintaining your weight. And, when the sun makes its solar return to Pisces on your birthday, and again as the sun enters Cancer (June 21-July 20), you'll lose the weight readily. For best results, start your weight loss program on the Thursday after a full moon.

When you do overeat, you usually do it in binges. When you feel a binge coming on call a friend or join Overeaters Anonymous. If you decide to go it alone, try lying on the floor, closing your eyes, and relaxing. Imagine yourself floating on a raft under the warm sun. Concentrate on the details of your imaginary scene—the color of the sky, the sound of the water, the feel of the breeze. If, after fifteen minutes of relaxation, you still feel like eating something, take three bites and then go on a thirty-minute brisk walk. Think about something other than food. If the craving is still there after all this, then give in—but don't feel guilty. You've probably walked the calories off anyway.

Since water retention is one of your biggest problems, your legs and feet swell. Meditating while you walk is a good exercise for swollen legs and feet. Francine, an in-the-know Piscean, walked herself from fat to thin. Her secret is moderation. She watches what and how much she eats. If she feels even the slightest tightness in her clothes, which she designs herself, she cuts down on her intake and increases her mileage. If you walked as much as Francine does, you could eat as much as you wanted without having to go on a strict diet. If walking doesn't appeal to you, try swimming, or scuba diving. Water is your second home, so relax and enjoy it.

The charts on the following pages will help you find the best time for *you* to lose weight. The easy-to-use astrological wheel has directions on setting up your chart by using your birthday. It shows you how to follow your sun's progress through your twelve houses. The Solar Transit Chart lets you record your weight loss as the sun moves from one house to the next. There is also a first week's menu that will allow you to include the foods you and your family love in your diet.

Familiarize yourself with the astrological wheel and the significance of each house as it pertains to the Pisces native.

The houses follow in a counterclockwise circle. Each house covers about a thirty-day period.

- When the Pisces sun transits your first house (Pisces), you want to enhance your appearance (weight loss).

- When the Pisces sun transits your second house (Aries), you want to indulge yourself (weight gain).

- When the Pisces sun transits your third house (Taurus), you are better able to express your ideas.

- When the Pisces sun transits your fourth house (Gemini), you want to nurture yourself (weight gain).

- When the Pisces sun transits your fifth house (Cancer), you achieve more confidence in yourself, your appearance, and your abilities (weight loss).

- When the Pisces sun transits your sixth house (Leo), you become more interested in your health and working conditions.

- When the Pisces sun transits your seventh house (Virgo), you form new relationships and your interest in others is renewed.

- When the Pisces sun transits your eighth house (Libra), you become interested in the resources of others as they affect you.

- When the Pisces sun transits your ninth house (Scorpio), you devise new plans for the future.

- When the Pisces sun transits your tenth house (Sagittarius), you move ahead with your career plans.

- When the Pisces sun transits your eleventh house (Capricorn), you want to cooperate in a group effort.

- When the Pisces sun transits your twelfth house

(Aquarius), you discover information previously unavailable to you.

• As the sun leaves your twelfth house and prepares to enter your first house again, you will be given a chance to reassess your last solar year and lay plans for the new year ahead.

To personalize your solar wheel insert your birthdate (month and day) in the blank space marked number 1 Pisces. Then moving counterclockwise, insert the next month and same day in the blank space marked number 2 Aries. Continue around the solar wheel, marking the month and day in the blank spaces until you come full circle.

You will now be able to follow the sun's transits through your horoscope and anticipate what areas of your life will be highlighted each thirty-day period. The transits will also tell you the times during the year dieting will be most successful. For those people born on the cusp of a sign (three days before or three days after) refer to the Solar Position Chart to find out what your sun really is.

To see how one dieter personalized his solar wheel, see page 29.

Solar Wheel Chart

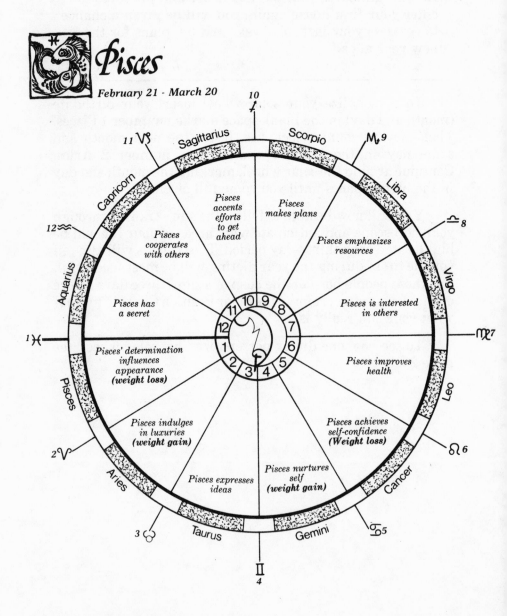

Pisces

February 21 - March 20

Pisces accents efforts to get ahead

Pisces makes plans

Pisces cooperates with others

Pisces emphasizes resources

Pisces has a secret

Pisces is interested in others

Pisces' determination influences appearance *(weight loss)*

Pisces improves health

Pisces indulges in luxuries *(weight gain)*

Pisces achieves self-confidence *(Weight loss)*

Pisces expresses ideas

Pisces nurtures self *(weight gain)*

The Solar Transit Chart provides you with a guide to those times of the year when you will lose weight and those times you will gain weight.

Insert your birthdate at the top of the chart in the space marked number 1 Pisces. Then insert the next month and same day in the space marked number 12 Aquarius. Continue across the top of the page until you reach number 12 Aquarius.

Record your total weight loss or gain with an X. At the end of the solar year, connect the Xs to reveal your astrological pattern.

To see how one dieter recorded her weight, see page 31.

Pisces Solar Transit Chart

Lbs.	Pisces	Aries	Taurus	Gemini	Cancer	Leo	Virgo	Libra	Scorpio	Sagittarius	Capricorn	Aquarius
House Numbers, Signs and Corresponding Dates												
10												
9												
8												
7												
6												
5												
4												
3												
2												
1												
-1												
-2												
-3												
-4												
-5												
-6												
-7												
-8												
-9												
-10												

The following diet allows 1200 calories a day for women, 1500 calories a day for men. I've tried to include foods Pisceans like in the menu plan. Since fluid retention is a problem for Pisces natives, I've recommended a one day only liquid diet to trigger initial weight loss. The liquid diet starts you out on the right foot by shrinking your stomach and flushing out your system. As the last common water sign in the zodiac, you'll find it easier to lose weight than either of your sister water signs.

Check substitutions and exchanges in the calorie/carbohydrate/protein counter in Appendix C. Once you've reached your desired weight (see Appendix A), increase your calorie intake gradually until you reach a level that lets you maintain that weight. Be sure to check with your doctor before beginning this or any other diet.

Recipes (marked with an asterisk) in this menu plan can be found in Chapter 15.

Pisces: First Day's Menu

Day One: Thursday

BREAKFAST
vegetable juice (any kind)
8 oz. milk
1 cup coffee or tea (with/without skim milk
    and 1 tsp. sugar), water

LUNCH
consommé
1 cup coffee or tea (with/without skim milk
    and 1 tsp. sugar), diet soda, water

DINNER
gazpacho*
vegetable juice (any kind)
jello made with fruit juice and topped with
    1 tbsp. cream
1 cup coffee or tea (with/without skim milk
    and 1 tsp. sugar), diet soda, water

Use this menu for one day only. Substitute any amount of juice, liquid, or soup for any of the items on the menu.

Day Two: Friday

BREAKFAST   Calories

open-face cheese sandwich on 1 slice whole wheat bread	165
½ grapefruit	45
strip bacon	42
coffee or tea (with/without skim milk and 1 tsp. sugar)	0-25

LUNCH

McDonald's cheeseburger	306
small french fries	211
iced tea, coffee, diet soda, water	0-25

DINNER

4 oz. spiced shrimp	108
¼ c. instant rice	45
cucumber	5
½ c. spinach salad and 1 strip crumbled bacon (1 tbsp. diet dressing)	91
1 small strawberry shortcake	170
coffee or tea (with/without skim milk and 1 tsp. sugar), diet soda, water	0-25
Total	1188-1263

Day Three: Saturday

BREAKFAST   Calories

½ grapefruit and 1 tbsp. honey	110
1 bran muffin and 1 pat butter	140
coffee or tea (with/without skim milk and 1 tsp. sugar)	0-25

LUNCH

1 c. crab salad on endive lettuce	155
1 c. vegetable beef soup	80
2 saltine crackers	25
3 oz. ice cream	100
iced tea, coffee, diet soda, water	0-25

DINNER

veal cutlet	185

½ baked potato with 1 pat butter (or 1
 tbsp. sour cream and chives) 110
1 c. green beans 30
½ c. steamed winter squash with
 Italian spices 65
1 glass rosé wine 85
coffee or tea (with/without skim milk and
 1 tsp. sugar), diet soda, water 0-25

Total	1085-1160

Day Four: Sunday

BREAKFAST   Calories
1 poached egg 100
1 slice toast with 1 pat butter 100
6 oz. apple juice 120
coffee or tea (with/without skim milk
 and 1 tsp. sugar) 0-25

LUNCH
fruit salad on lettuce leaf 126
½ c. cheese mixed with raisins and dates . 200
1 blueberry muffin and 1 pat butter 145
iced tea, coffee, diet soda, water 0-25

DINNER
2 crackers 25
1 lb. lobster with 1 tbsp. butter 212
½ c. fresh steamed asparagus with
 almonds 40
mixed green salad (1 tbsp. diet dressing) . 60
1 glass white wine 85
coffee or tea (with/without skim milk
 and 1 tsp. sugar), diet soda, water 0-25

Total	1213-1288

Day Five: Monday

BREAKFAST Calories

½ c. oatmeal (with ½ c. skim milk and
  1 tsp. sugar) 104
8 oz. orange juice....................... 120
1 cup coffee or tea (with/without skim
  milk and 1 tsp. sugar)................. 0-25

LUNCH

1 c. clam chowder 100
lettuce and tomato salad (1 tbsp.
  diet dressing)......................... 60
1 apple and 1 oz. cheese 180
iced tea, coffee, diet soda, water.......... 0-25

DINNER

Indian chicken* 245
½ c. instant rice 90
½ c. carrots and 1 pat butter 60
¼ c. cantaloupe with ½ c. fresh strawberries over 2 oz. vanilla ice cream 125
1 cup coffee or tea (with/without skim milk
  and 1 tsp. sugar), diet soda, water 0-25

Total   1084-
1159

Day Six: Tuesday

BREAKFAST Calories

6 oz. cranberry juice 123
1 egg cooked any way 100
1 slice of toast with 1 pat butter.......... 100
1 cup coffee or tea (with/without skim
  milk and 1 tsp. sugar)................. 0-25

LUNCH

½ c. tuna salad with fruit and vegetables . 200
2 saltine crackers 25
iced tea, coffee, diet soda, water.......... 0-25

DINNER

2 oz. fish sticks...........................	100
1 c. macaroni and cheese	430
½ c. fresh steamed broccoli with with 1 pat butter	55
lettuce wedge and 1 tbsp. diet dressing...	30
coffee or tea (with/without skim milk and 1 tsp. sugar), diet soda, water	0-25
Total	1163-1238

Day Seven: Wednesday

BREAKFAST   Calories

¼ cantaloupe	40
yogurt shake	135
coffee or tea (with/without skim milk and 1 tsp. sugar).....................	0-25

LUNCH

open-face turkey sandwich	185
1 tbsp. cranberry sauce.................	25
lettuce and tomato salad (1 tbsp. diet dressing).........................	60
iced tea, coffee, diet soda, water..........	0-25
dessert (your choice)....................	200

DINNER

New England style fish*................	180
1 baked potato with 1 pat butter and 1 slice bacon crumbled	152
mixed fresh vegetables steamed..........	45
1 fried banana and 1 tbsp. whipped cream	145
coffee or tea (with/without skim milk and 1 tsp. sugar), diet soda, water	0-25
Total	1167-1242

Chapter 15

Quick & Simple

Some astrological signs love to cook, and some don't. Some are good cooks, some aren't. The low calorie and low carbohydrate recipes in this chapter are for both kinds, and the recipes range from soup to nuts. They're purposely made quick and simple, to keep you out of the kitchen and encourage your interest in other things besides food. The less time you spend preparing a meal, the less tempted you are to overeat. Use the recipes in your menu planner or experiment with new and unusual combinations. It's easy to substitute one ingredient for another, so go ahead.

If you're the chief cook and bottle washer in the family, it's up to you to see that they get nutritious, appetizing, unfattening meals with the minimum amount of fuss. If, on the other hand, you're responsible only for yourself, then it's up to you to make yourself attractive meals that meet all of your body's nutritional requirements without gaining weight. With the recipes in this chapter, you'll cut down on preparation and cleanup time.

If you're interested in dieting, chances are you have looked at other diet recipes. In researching different recipes, I found many of the so-called "diet" recipes have more calories or carbohydrates than the non-diet version. Check over some of those old family favorites. See if they're really high in calories or carbohydrates, or if you can cut down on either by substituting one ingredient for another. You may be pleasantly surprised.

The following recipes are from the menu planners for each of the signs, but they can be used by anyone. We've tried to give you recipes that are easy to follow, and are made with relatively inexpensive, readily available ingredients. Some of the dishes are stir-fried or highly seasoned for those signs that like exotic food and need a little something different in their diets.

Many diets with weekly menus feature different foods every day, so you have little chance to use your leftovers. In the suggested menu plan, we suggest a number of interesting ways to disguise your leftovers. No one will ever be the wiser.

Calorie/carbohydrate counts may vary from brand to brand. Most of the recipes in *Diet Signs* use the brand name products with the lowest calories/carbohydrates count we could find. Shop and compare. You may be surprised to find where you can cut down.

Aries

Chicken in Basket *(8 Carbohydrates)*

    1 slice bread
    1 egg
    1 pat butter

1. Cut out center of bread with cookie cutter or small glass
2. Melt butter in heavy skillet.

3. Add slice of bread to skillet.
4. Break egg in center of hole. Fry until brown.
5. Flip toast to other side and brown.

Serves 1

Lamb Curry *(8 carbohydrates)*

    1 lb. lamb, cubed
    ¼ cup cooking oil
    2 onions, chopped
    2 tart apples, peeled and chopped
    2 teaspoons curry powder
    ½ teaspoon salt
    ¼ teaspoon pepper
    ¼ teaspoon cinnamon
    1 cup bouillon

1. Heat the oil in a heavy skillet and add the lamb. Brown. Remove to a plate.
2. Add the onions and apples to the drippings and cook over low heat with cover on until it becomes soft. Stir occasionally.
3. Add curry powder, salt, pepper, and cinnamon to apples and mix.
4. Add bouillon, stir, and bring to a boil. Add the lamb and reduce heat.
5. Cover and simmer over low heat for 30 minutes until meat is tender. Serve immediately over hot rice or noodles.

Serves 6

Chili *(9 carbohydrates)*

    1 tablespoon cooking oil
    ½ lb. coarsely-ground, ground chuck
    1 onion, chopped

1 red pepper, chopped
1 can (8 oz.) peeled tomatoes
1 teaspoon chili powder or to taste
¼ teaspoon salt
pepper to taste

1. Heat oil in a pan. Sauté the ground chuck, onion, and red
   pepper together until browned.
2. Drain off any fat.
3. Add tomatoes, chili powder, salt, and pepper to the cooked
   meat.
4. Bring to a boil, cover, reduce heat, and simmer for 1 hour
   until the sauce begins to thicken. Stir occasionally.

Serve over rice or beans. This recipe may be prepared ahead of
time and frozen.

Serves 2 (approx.)

Stir-Fried Broccoli
Beef (8 carbohydrates)

¾ lb. top round steak, thinly sliced across the grain
2 cups broccoli, cut into bite-sized pieces
½ cup celery, sliced thin on the diagonal
1 onion, cut into wedges
2 clove garlic, minced
1 teaspoon cornstarch
¼ teaspoon salt
2 tablespoons soy sauce
2 tablespoons sherry
2 tablespoons cooking oil

1. Mix the cornstarch, salt, soy sauce, and sherry together. Add the
   meat and marinate 15 to 30 minutes.
2. Heat oil in a heavy skillet or wok. Add meat and garlic and
   stir-fry for 3 minutes.

3. Add the broccoli, celery, and onion to the meat and continue to stir-fry 3 more minutes or until vegetables are hot and crispy.
4. In a bowl, mix ¼ cup water and 1 teaspoon cornstarch and add to the broccoli and beef. Stir until the sauce thickens.

Serve immediately over hot rice or lo mein noodles.

Serves 4

Taurus

Yogurt Shake *(Approx. 135 calories)*

1 cup skim milk
½ cup strawberries, peaches, apricots, raspberries or pineapple
½ cup plain low calorie yogurt
6-8 ice cubes
1 teaspoon lemon juice

1. Put all of the above ingredients in a blender and whip until creamy.

Serves 4

Mock Melba *(88 calories)*

1 fresh peach, peeled and sliced
½ cup red raspberries, blackberries, or boysenberries
½ teaspoon lemon juice
1 teaspoon sugar

1. Place the berries, lemon juice, and sugar in a blender and whip for 30 seconds.
2. Place the peach slices in a dessert dish and spoon berries over them.

Serves 1

Cube Steak with Peppers and Tomato *(260 calories)*

1 lb. cubed steak
1 tablespoon cooking oil
1 can (1 lb.) stewed tomatoes
¼ cup sliced onions
1 clove garlic, crushed
1 tablespoon cornstarch
1 green pepper, seeded and sliced
dash of red wine to taste

1. Fry the steak in oil until it is cooked to your liking.
2. Remove steak to a serving dish.
3. Add tomatoes, onions, green peppers, garlic, and wine to the pan drippings. Heat.
4. Mix ⅛ cup water and cornstarch and add to the heated pan drippings. Stir over low heat until sauce begins to thicken.
5. Add steak to sauce.
Sprinkle with grated cheese and serve.

Serves 4

Gemini

Stuffed Celery *(40 calories)*

10 stalks of celery
1 teaspoon sugar
½ cup diet cottage cheese
½ peeled carrot
1 tablespoon minced parsley
2 tablespoons minced chives
seasoned salt
caraway seeds

1. Submerge celery in sugared ice water for 30 minutes to one hour prior to stuffing.
2. Grate 1 stalk of celery and carrot together.
3. Blend cottage cheese, celery, carrot, parsley, and chives.
4. Cut the remaining celery stalks into 3″ pieces.
5. Spread 1½ teaspoons of cottage cheese in the center of each piece of celery.
6. Sprinkle with seasoned salt and caraway seeds.

This recipe can be made ahead and refrigerated.

Serves 4

Stir-Fried Chicken, Cauliflower and Carrots *(289 calories)*

2 tablespoons oil
2 cups chicken, skinned and cubed
1 cup water
2 tablespoons cornstarch
1 tablespoon soy sauce
1 tablespoon sherry
1 tablespoon sugar
1 tablespoon chicken-flavored instant bouillon
1 cup carrots, sliced diagonally
1 medium onion, sliced into thin wedges
1 cup fresh cauliflower, cut into bite-size flowerets

1. Heat oil in a heavy skillet or wok.
2. Add chicken and stir-fry 3 minutes until tender.
3. Add carrots, onion, and cauliflower and continue stirring for 3 more minutes until heated through and crispy.
4. Mix cornstarch, soy sauce, sherry, sugar and bouillon in water.
5. Mix cornstarch mixture to chicken and vegetables and stir until thickened.
6. Serve hot over rice or chow mein.

Serves 4

Vegetable Omelette *(260 calories)*

4 eggs
2 teaspoons water
2 tablespoons butter or margarine
1 small zucchini, sliced thin
⅛ lb. fresh mushrooms, sliced
¼ cup onions, sliced
1 fresh tomato, peeled and chopped
1 teaspoon oregano

Vegetables
1. Melt 1 tablespoon butter in a saucepan and add the zucchini, mushrooms, onions, tomato, and oregano.
2. Sauté over low heat for 4 minutes. Set aside.

Omelette
1. Beat the eggs with water for 1 minute with fork or wire whisk.
2. Melt butter in an omlette pan or skillet. Add half the eggs and cover. Cook over low heat until the top is dry.
3. Place half the vegetables in the center of the omelette and fold one side over the other.
4. Repeat steps 1 through 3.
Serve while hot with a dash of parmesan or romano cheese.

Serves 2

Cancer

Shrimp with Almonds *(245 calories)*

3 tablespoons butter or margarine
¼ cup slivered or sliced almonds
2 lbs. shrimp, shelled and de-veined
¼ teaspoon salt

2 tablespoons chopped chives
pepper to taste

1. Melt 1 tablespoon butter in a saucepan and sauté the almonds until golden brown. Remove to a serving dish.
2. In the same pan, melt 1 more tablespoon butter and sauté 1 pound of shrimp until pink and tender. Remove and add to the almonds.
3. Repeat step number 2.
4. Add the salt, pepper, and chives and toss lightly with the shrimp and almonds.

Serve while hot with rice pilaf and garnish with a twist of lemon.

Serves 4

Broccoli with Cheese *(160 calories)*

1 lb. fresh broccoli
1 tablespoon butter or margarine
1 tablespoon flour
1 tablespoon prepared mustard
1 cup skim milk
1 cup shredded cheese

1. Clean and cut the broccoli into spears and steam until tender.
2. Arrange the broccoli spears on a serving plate.
3. Melt the butter in a pan and stir in the flour and mustard. Add the milk and stir until the sauce thickens. Add the cheese and fold in gently until the sauce is well-blended and cheese is completely melted.
4. Pour cheese sauce over broccoil and garnish with a twist of lemon or orange.

Serves 4

Individual Cheesecake *(170 calories)*

24 oz. package cream cheese
1 cup sugar
5 eggs
1½ teaspoons vanilla extract
1 cup sour cream
¼ cup sugar
1 can (1 lb.) cherry, pineapple, or blueberry pie filling

1. Cream together eggs and cream cheese, adding eggs one at a time.
2. Add 1 cup of sugar and the vanilla to the cream cheese.
3. Pour the mixture into paper muffin cups.
4. Bake in 300 degree oven for 25 minutes or until the tops begin to crack.
5. Mix the sour cream and ¼ cup sugar together and spread over the cheesecakes.
6. Return the cakes to oven for 5 more minutes.
7. When cool, top with pie filling and refrigerate.

This recipe may be made ahead and refrigerated.

Serves 30

Leo

Hot Lemonade *(8 carbohydrates)*

6 oz. hot water
½ freshly squeezed lemon
1 teaspoon honey

1. Pour the hot water over freshly squeezed lemon juice; add honey and stir.

Serve while hot.

Serves 1

Florida Cocktail *(18 carbohydrates)*

6 oz. grapefruit juice

1. Serve the grapefruit juice over ice and garnish with a twist of lime and a sprig of mint.

Serves 1

Hawaiian Chicken *(11 carbohydrates)*

2 lbs. chicken, skinned
1 can (8 oz.) pineapple
1 teaspoon onion, minced
1 tablespoon lemon juice
1½ teaspoons cornstarch
dash of salt
ground ginger

1. Arrange chicken in a baking pan.
2. Drain pineapple and set the juice aside.
3. Mix the pineapple juice, 1 teaspoon cornstarch, onion, and salt and poor over chicken.
4. Bake chicken in 375 degree oven for 50 minutes or until tender. Remove to serving dish.
5. In a pan, combine pineapple juice, lemon juice, cornstarch, and ginger. Stir over low heat until sauce thickens.
6. Add pineapple and heat through.
7. Serve pineapple and sauce over chicken and sprinkle with flaked coconut.

Serves 4

Ambrosia *(21 carbohydrates)*

2 oranges, peeled and sectioned
2 cups fresh pineapple chunks
⅓ cup maraschino cherry halves
⅓ cup coconut, shredded

1. Combine oranges, pineapple, cherries and coconut. Toss lightly and chill.
This recipe may be made ahead and refrigerated.

Serves 4

Virgo

California Tuna Salad *(200 calories)*

¼ grapefruit
½ orange
1 tablespoon wine vinegar
1 teaspoon sugar
¼ cup sliced onions
2 pitted black olives, sliced
1 can (3½ oz.) water-packed tuna
1 cup lettuce leaves

1. Peel and section grapefruit and orange.
2. Add vinegar, sugar, onion, olives, and tuna and toss.
3. Marinate in the refrigerator 1 hour before serving.
4. Add lettuce leaves, toss, and serve.
This recipe can be made ahead of serving time up to 8 hours before eating.

Serves 1

Carob Drink *(88 calories)*

2 oz. carob powder
2 oz. water
pinch of salt
2⅓ cups skim milk
2 tablespoons fructose
⅓ teaspoon vanilla extract

1. In a saucepan, combine carob, water, and salt. Bring to a boil. Stir syrup occasionally.
2. Add milk and fructose to syrup and continue to stir. Heat but do not boil.
3. Add vanilla and beat in with a wire whisk.
Can be served hot or cold.

Serves 4

Buttermilk Dressing *(7 calories per tbsp.)*

1 cup buttermilk
2 teaspoons onion powder
1 teaspoon garlic powder
4 teaspoons lemon juice
1 teaspoon parsley flakes
2 teaspoons chopped chives
1 teaspoon sugar

1. Combine all, and shake well.
2. Serve with a green salad.
Keep refrigerated.

Serves 4

Libra

Salad Dressing *(10 calories per tbsp.)*

 1 can (10¾ oz.) condensed tomato soup
 3-4 tablespoons vinegar
 1 clove garlic, finely chopped
 1 teaspoon onion salt
 pepper to taste

1. Combine all the ingredients and shake until well blended.
2. Serve with a green salad.
Keep refrigerated.

 Serves 4

Meaty Rice *(120 calories)*

 1 beef bouillon cube
 1 tablespoon butter or margarine
 ½ cup long grain rice
 2 scallions, chopped
 ½ teaspoon salt
 ¼ teaspoon pepper
 ⅛ teaspoon thyme
 ½ cup celery, chopped
 dash of wine to taste

1. Melt butter and sauté rice until golden brown.
2. Place rice in a casserole dish.
3. Dissolve bouillon cube in 1¼ cups water and add wine to taste.
4. Add the bouillon and remaining ingredients to the rice and bake in a 350-degree oven for 40 minutes.
Serve while hot.

 Serves 4

Steak and Tomatoes *(260 calories)*

1 lb. cubed steak
1 tablespoon cooking oil
¼ cup water
3 peeled tomatoes
¼ cup sliced onions
1 tablespoon sugar
1 teaspoon basil
1 tablespoon cornstarch
salt to taste

1. Fry the steak in oil until it is cooked to your liking.
2. Remove steak to a serving platter.
3. Add ⅛ cup of water, 2 chopped tomatoes, onion slices, basil, and salt to the pan drippings. Heat.
4. Mix remaining water with cornstarch and add to the heated drippings. Continue to stir over low heat until sauce begins to thicken.
5. Slice the remaining tomato and add both tomato and steak to the sauce. Toss lightly.
Serve immediately.

Serves 4

Scorpio

Fruit Soup *(100 calories)*

½ cup raspberries, crushed
½ cup orange juice
¼ cup sugar
½ cup peaches, peeled

1. Combine all ingredients in a saucepan and simmer 10 minutes.
2. Allow to cool and mix in blender at high speed for 30 seconds.
Garnish with a slice of lemon or orange and serve cold.

Serves 2

Spicy Shrimp *(245 calories)*

1 lb. shrimp, shelled and de-veined
1 tablespoon cooking oil
2 tablespoons soy sauce
2 tablespoons vinegar
2 tablespoons ketchup
2 teaspoons sugar
½ teaspoon ginger
½ teaspoon garlic salt
2 chopped scallions

1. Heat cooking oil and sauté shrimp until pink and tender.
2. Add the remaining ingredients to shrimp and simmer for 5 more minutes until heated through.

Serve immediately over rice or noodles.

Serves 4

Spaghetti Squash and Clams *(109 calories)*

1 spaghetti squash
2-6½ oz. cans chopped clams
½ oz. dry butter substitute
2 cloves garlic, minced
¼ cup parsley, chopped
¼ cup romano cheese
pepper to taste

1. Steam spaghetti squash for 20 minutes or until tender and easy to shred. Remove spaghetti from squash and place on a serving dish.
2. Sprinkle with cheese and toss.
3. Drain clams and reserve the clam juice.

4. In a saucepan, mix clam juice, dry butter substitute, garlic, salt, and pepper until heated. Add clams and parsley, then pour over spaghetti and cheese.

Serves 4

Sagittarius

Potato Salad *(12 carbohydrates)*

   4 potatoes, cooked and cubed
   2 eggs, hard-boiled and chopped
   ¼ cup salad dressing
   1 tablespoon prepared mustard
   2 tablespoons onion, minced
   2 tablespoons bacon bits
   1 teaspoon salt
   pepper to taste

1. Combine potatoes, eggs, onions, bacon bits, salt, and pepper. Toss lightly.
2. Blend salad dressing and mustard. Combine with potato mixture and refrigerate.
This recipe may be made ahead and refrigerated.

Serves 4

Tuna Salad with Vegetables *(6 carbohydrates)*

   1 can (6½ oz.) water-packed tuna
   1 cucumber, thinly sliced

½ cup chopped celery
¼ cup grated carrot
1 tablespoon minced onion
½ cup vinegar
1 teaspoon salad herbs
1 teaspoon sugar
2 tablespoons toasted sesame seeds
¼ teaspoon salt
fresh lettuce leaves

1. Combine vinegar, herbs, sugar, 1 tablespoon sesame seeds, and salt. Shake and set aside.
2. In a bowl, combine cucumber, celery, carrots, and onion and toss with salad dressing. Refrigerate for at least 1 hour.
3. Drain the tuna and divide in half.
4. Line two plates with lettuce leaves and mold half the tuna in the center of each plate.
5. Arrange marinated vegetables around the tuna and sprinkle the remaining sesame seeds on top.

This recipe may be made ahead and refrigerated.

Serves 2

Mexican Chicken *(9 carbohydrates)*

4 chicken breasts (1-1½ lbs.)
2 tablespoons flour
2 tablespoons oil
1 can (8 oz.) tomato sauce
1 tablespoon sugar
1 tablespoon parsley
1 teaspoon salt
½-1 teaspoon chili powder
1 oz. cheddar cheese, grated

1. Remove skin and fat from chicken.
2. Roll chicken in flour.

3. Heat oil and add chicken.
4. Sauté chicken breasts for 5 minutes on each side.
5. Add tomato sauce, sugar, parsley, salt, and chili powder. Simmer for 20 minutes.
6. Sprinkle with grated cheese before serving.

Serves 4

Capricorn

Onions, Steak, and Mushrooms *(330 calories)*

1 lb. round steak
2 tablespoons cornstarch
2 tablespoons soy sauce
2 tablespoons sherry
½ teaspoon sugar
2 tablespoons oil
3 cups sliced onions
¼-½ lb. mushrooms, sliced

1. Slice steak into ¼″ wide strips.
2. In a bowl, mix cornstarch, soy sauce, sherry, and sugar.
3. Add meat and marinate for 15 minutes.
4. Heat oil in a skillet, add meat and stir constantly 3 to 5 minutes.
5. Add onions and mushrooms and continue to stir another 3 to 5 minutes.

Serves 4

Spinach Salad *(160 calories)*

2 cups raw spinach, torn into small pieces

¼ cup sliced fresh mushrooms
1 hard-boiled egg, chopped
¼ cup sliced onion
1 tablespoon bacon bits
¼ cup low calorie Italian dressing

1. Combine spinach, cheese, mushrooms, egg, onions, and bacon bits into a serving bowl and toss lightly.
2. Add dressing before serving.

Serves 2

Double-Baked Potato *(100 calories)*

1 baked potato
½ cup low fat cottage cheese
1 teaspoon chopped chives
1 tablespoon grated cheese

1. Cut the baked potato in half, lengthwise.
2. Scoop the potato out of its shell and mash with the cottage cheese and chives.
3. Refill shell with the mashed potatoes.
4. Top with grated cheese and return the potatoes to the oven and heat through and melt the cheese.
Serve while hot.

Serves 2

Aquarius

Hawaiian Breakfast Drink *(96 calories)*

1 cup plain yogurt
½ cup skim milk
1 banana
1 tablespoon honey
1 tablespoon coconut
2 tablespoons orange juice concentrate
8 ice cubes

1. Combine all ingredients in a blender and whip until smooth and creamy.

Serves 4

Shrimp and Snow Peas *(200 calories)*

1 lb. fresh or frozen snow peas
1 lb. unshelled shrimp, frozen or fresh
½ cup chicken broth
1 tablespoon sherry
1 tablespoon cornstarch
⅛ teaspoon ground ginger

1. Clean and trim snow peas.
2. Blanch in boiling water for 2-3 minutes.
3. Rinse and drain in cold water.
4. Heat oil in heavy skillet or wok, add shrimp and stir fry for 3 minutes or until pink.
5. Add snow peas and ginger.
6. Stir-fry for 2 minutes until hot and crispy.
7. In a bowl mix broth, sherry, and cornstarch and add to shrimp and snow peas. Stir until the sauce thickens.
8. Serve over hot fluffy rice.

Serves 4

Orange Breakfast
Drink *(260 calories)*

2 eggs
¼ cup frozen orange juice concentrate
1 tablespoon honey
1¼ cups cold milk

1. Combine eggs, orange juice and honey in a blender.
2. Gradually add the cold milk and whip at high speed for 30
   seconds until frothy.

   Serves 2

Pisces

New England Style Fish *(180 calories)*

4 flounder filets, fresh or frozen (or any fish)
1 can (10½ oz.) clam chowder
½ cup skim milk

1. Heat milk and chowder in a saucepan.
2. Pour ¼ of chowder into a casserole dish.
3. Roll up fillets and place in the casserole dish.
4. Pour the rest of the chowder over filets.
5. Bake for 18 minutes or until filet is tender in a 375-degree oven.
6. Serve with a twist of lemon and a sprig of parsley.

   Serves 4

Gazpacho *(70 calories)*

    1 cucumber, peeled and diced
    1 small green pepper, seeded and diced
    2 cups tomato juice
    1 small onion, peeled and diced
    wine vinegar to taste
    Italian spices to taste
    dash tobasco sauce

1. Blend cucumber, tomato juice, pepper, and onion on high speed for 1 minute or until smooth.
2. Season to taste and blend for 10 seconds more.
3. Serve over crushed ice with a twist of raw cucumber.

Serves 4

Indian Chicken *(245 calories)*

    1 lb. chicken breasts, skinned
    6 tablespoons lemon juice
    ½ teaspoon paprika
    ½ teaspoon salt
    1 cup plain yogurt
    1 tablespoon honey
    1 teaspoon grated lemon rind
    2 teaspoon flour
    1 teaspoon ground ginger
    2 cloves garlic, crushed

1. Arrange chicken breasts in a casserole or baking dish.
2. Sprinkle the chicken with 4 tablespoons of lemon juice, salt, and paprika.
3. Bake in 350-degree oven for 40 minutes or until tender.
4. Combine the remaining ingredients in a bowl and spoon over the chicken. Bake 5 minutes more.

Serve while hot and garnish with a twist of lemon.

Serves 4

Appendix A.

Desirable Weights*
Men 25 and Older

Weight in Pounds (clothed)

Height (with 1" heels)				
Feet	Inches	Small Frame	Medium Frame	Large Frame
5	2	112-120	118-129	126-141
5	3	115-123	121-133	129-144
5	4	118-126	124-136	132-148
5	5	121-129	127-139	135-152
5	6	124-133	130-143	138-156
5	7	128-137	134-147	142-161
5	8	132-141	138-152	147-166
5	9	136-145	142-156	151-170
5	10	140-150	146-160	155-174
5	11	144-154	150-165	159-179
6	0	148-158	154-170	164-184
6	1	152-162	158-175	168-189
6	2	156-167	162-180	173-194
6	3	160-171	167-185	178-199
6	4	164-175	172-190	182-204

*Based on new statistical studies, revised weight tables are being formulated. The updated desirable weights for men and women today are probably higher than those in the table above, which were based on statistical studies made 25 years ago. *Courtesy of the Metropolitan Life Insurance Company.*

Desirable Weights*
Women 25 and Older
(For girls between ages 18 and 25,
subtract one pound for each year under 25.)

| Height (with 2″ heels) | | Weight in Pounds (clothed) | | |
Feet	Inches	Small Frame	Medium Frame	Large Frame
4	10	92-98	96-107	104-119
4	11	94-101	98-110	106-122
5	0	96-104	101-113	109-125
5	1	99-107	104-116	112-128
5	2	102-110	107-119	115-131
5	3	105-113	110-122	118-134
5	4	108-116	113-126	121-138
5	5	111-119	116-130	125-142
5	6	114-123	120-135	129-146
5	7	118-127	124-139	133-150
5	8	122-131	128-143	137-154
5	9	126-135	132-147	141-158
5	10	130-140	136-151	145-163
5	11	134-144	140-155	149-168
6	0	138-148	144-159	153-173

*Based on new statistical studies, revised weight tables are being formulated. The updated desirable weights for men and women today are probably higher than those in the table above, which were based on statistical studies made 25 years ago. *Courtesy of the Metropolitan Life Insurance Company.*

Appendix B

Solar Position Chart
(1900-1999 A.D.)

The beginning dates of each sign of the zodiac are listed by year

	1900	1901	1902	1903	1904
Aquarius	Jan. 20	Jan. 21	Jan. 21	Jan. 21	Jan. 21
Pisces	Feb. 19	Feb. 19	Feb. 20	Feb. 20	Feb. 20
Aries	Mar. 21	Mar. 21	Mar. 22	Mar. 22	Mar. 21
Taurus	April 21	April 21	April 21	April 21	April 21
Gemini	May 22	May 22	May 22	May 22	May 22
Cancer	June 22	June 22	June 22	June 23	June 22
Leo	July 23	July 24	July 24	July 24	July 23
Virgo	Aug. 24	Aug. 24	Aug. 24	Aug. 24	Aug. 24
Libra	Sept. 24	Sept. 24	Sept. 24	Sept. 24	Sept. 23
Scorpio	Oct. 24	Oct. 24	Oct. 24	Oct. 25	Oct. 24
Sagittarius	Nov. 23	Nov. 23	Nov. 23	Nov. 23	Nov. 23
Capricorn	Dec. 22	Dec. 23	Dec. 23	Dec. 23	Dec. 22

	1905	1906	1907	1908	1909
Aquarius	Jan. 21	Jan. 21	Jan. 21	Jan. 21	Jan. 21
Pisces	Feb. 19	Feb. 20	Feb. 20	Feb. 20	Feb. 19
Aries	Mar. 21	Mar. 22	Mar. 22	Mar. 21	Mar. 21
Taurus	April 21	April 21	April 21	April 21	April 21
Gemini	May 22	May 22	May 22	May 21	May 22
Cancer	June 22	June 22	June 23	June 22	June 22
Leo	July 24	July 24	July 24	July 23	July 24
Virgo	Aug. 24	Aug. 24	Aug. 24	Aug. 24	Aug. 24
Libra	Sept. 24	Sept. 24	Sept. 24	Sept. 23	Sept. 24
Scorpio	Oct. 24	Oct. 24	Oct. 25	Oct. 24	Oct. 24
Sagittarius	Nov. 23	Nov. 23	Nov. 23	Nov. 23	Nov. 23
Capricorn	Dec. 23	Dec. 23	Dec. 23	Dec. 22	Dec. 22

212

	1910	1911	1912	1913	1914
Aquarius	Jan. 21	Jan. 21	Jan. 21	Jan. 21	Jan. 21
Pisces	Feb. 20	Feb. 20	Feb. 20	Feb. 19	Feb. 19
Aries	Mar. 22	Mar. 22	Mar. 21	Mar. 21	Mar. 21
Taurus	April 21	April 21	April 20	April 21	April 21
Gemini	May 22	May 22	May 21	May 22	May 22
Cancer	June 22	June 23	June 22	June 22	June 22
Leo	July 24	July 24	July 23	July 24	July 24
Virgo	Aug. 24	Aug. 24	Aug. 24	Aug. 24	Aug. 24
Libra	Sept. 24	Sept. 24	Sept. 23	Sept. 24	Sept. 24
Scorpio	Oct. 24	Oct. 25	Oct. 24	Oct. 24	Oct. 24
Sagittarius	Nov. 23	Nov. 23	Nov. 23	Nov. 23	Nov. 23
Capricorn	Dec. 23	Dec. 23	Dec. 22	Dec. 22	Dec. 23

	1915	1916	1917	1918	1919
Aquarius	Jan. 21	Jan. 21	Jan. 21	Jan. 21	Jan. 21
Pisces	Feb. 20	Feb. 20	Feb. 19	Feb. 19	Feb. 20
Aries	Mar. 22	Mar. 21	Mar. 21	Mar. 21	Mar. 22
Taurus	April 21	April 20	April 21	April 21	April 21
Gemini	May 22	May 21	May 22	May 22	May 22
Cancer	June 23	June 22	June 22	June 22	June 22
Leo	July 24	July 23	July 23	July 24	July 24
Virgo	Aug. 24	Aug. 24	Aug. 24	Aug. 24	Aug. 24
Libra	Sept. 24	Sept. 23	Sept. 24	Sept. 24	Sept. 24
Scorpio	Oct. 25	Oct. 24	Oct. 24	Oct. 25	Oct. 24
Sagittarius	Nov. 23	Nov. 23	Nov. 23	Nov. 23	Nov. 23
Capricorn	Dec. 23	Dec. 22	Dec. 22	Dec. 23	Dec. 23

	1920	1921	1922	1923	1924
Aquarius	Jan. 21	Jan. 21	Jan. 21	Jan. 21	Jan. 21
Pisces	Feb. 20	Feb. 19	Feb. 19	Feb. 20	Feb. 20
Aries	Mar. 21	Mar. 21	Mar. 21	Mar. 22	Mar. 21
Taurus	April 21	April 21	April 21	April 22	April 21
Gemini	May 21	May 22	May 22	May 22	May 21
Cancer	June 22	June 22	June 22	June 22	June 22
Leo	July 23	July 23	July 24	July 24	July 23
Virgo	Aug. 23	Aug. 24	Aug. 24	Aug. 24	Aug. 23
Libra	Sept. 23	Sept. 24	Sept. 24	Sept. 24	Sept. 23
Scorpio	Oct. 24	Oct. 24	Oct. 24	Oct. 24	Oct. 24
Sagittarius	Nov. 23	Nov. 23	Nov. 23	Nov. 23	Nov. 23
Capricorn	Dec. 22	Dec. 22	Dec. 23	Dec. 23	Dec. 22

	1925	1926	1927	1928	1929
Aquarius	Jan. 21	Jan. 21	Jan. 21	Jan. 21	Jan. 21
Pisces	Feb. 19	Feb. 19	Feb. 20	Feb. 20	Feb. 19
Aries	Mar. 21	Mar. 21	Mar. 22	Mar. 21	Mar. 21
Taurus	April 21	April 21	April 21	April 20	April 21
Gemini	May 22	May 22	May 22	May 21	May 22
Cancer	June 22	June 22	June 22	June 22	June 22
Leo	July 23	July 24	July 24	July 23	July 23
Virgo	Aug. 24	Aug. 24	Aug. 24	Aug. 23	Aug. 24
Libra	Sept. 24	Sept. 24	Sept. 24	Sept. 23	Sept. 24
Scorpio	Oct. 24	Oct. 24	Oct. 24	Oct. 24	Oct. 24
Sagittarius	Nov. 23	Nov. 23	Nov. 23	Nov. 23	Nov. 23
Capricorn	Dec. 22	Dec. 23	Dec. 23	Dec. 22	Dec. 22

	1930	1931	1932	1933	1934
Aquarius	Jan. 21	Jan. 21	Jan. 21	Jan. 20	Jan. 21
Pisces	Feb. 19	Feb. 20	Feb. 20	Feb. 19	Feb. 19
Aries	Mar. 21	Mar. 22	Mar. 21	Mar. 21	Mar. 21
Taurus	April 21	April 21	April 20	April 21	April 21
Gemini	May 22	May 22	May 21	May 22	May 22
Cancer	June 22	June 22	June 22	June 22	June 22
Leo	July 24	July 24	July 23	July 23	July 24
Virgo	Aug. 24	Aug. 24	Aug. 23	Aug. 24	Aug. 24
Libra	Sept. 24	Sept. 24	Sept. 23	Sept. 24	Sept. 24
Scorpio	Oct. 24	Oct. 24	Oct. 24	Oct. 24	Oct. 24
Sagittarius	Nov. 23	Nov. 23	Nov. 23	Nov. 23	Nov. 23
Capricorn	Dec. 23	Dec. 23	Dec. 22	Dec. 22	Dec. 23

	1935	1936	1937	1938	1939
Aquarius	Jan. 21	Jan. 21	Jan. 20	Jan. 21	Jan. 21
Pisces	Feb. 20	Feb. 20	Feb. 19	Feb. 19	Feb. 20
Aries	Mar. 22	Mar. 21	Mar. 21	Mar. 21	Mar. 22
Taurus	April 21	April 20	April 21	April 21	April 21
Gemini	May 22	May 21	May 21	May 22	May 22
Cancer	June 22	June 22	June 22	June 22	June 22
Leo	July 24	July 23	July 23	July 24	July 24
Virgo	Aug. 24	Aug. 23	Aug. 24	Aug. 24	Aug. 24
Libra	Sept. 24	Sept. 23	Sept. 23	Sept. 24	Sept. 24
Scorpio	Oct. 24	Oct. 24	Oct. 24	Oct. 24	Oct. 24
Sagittarius	Nov. 23	Nov. 22	Nov. 23	Nov. 23	Nov. 23
Capricorn	Dec. 23	Dec. 22	Dec. 22	Dec. 23	Dec. 22

	1940	1941	1942	1943	1944
Aquarius	Jan. 21	Jan. 20	Jan. 21	Jan. 21	Jan. 21
Pisces	Feb. 20	Feb. 19	Feb. 19	Feb. 20	Feb. 20
Aries	Mar. 21	Mar. 21	Mar. 21	Mar. 22	Mar. 21
Taurus	April 20	April 20	April 21	April 21	April 20
Gemini	May 21	May 21	May 22	May 22	May 21
Cancer	June 22	June 22	June 22	June 22	June 22
Leo	July 23	July 23	July 24	July 24	July 23
Virgo	Aug. 23	Aug. 24	Aug. 24	Aug. 24	Aug. 23
Libra	Sept. 23	Sept. 23	Sept. 24	Sept. 24	Sept. 23
Scorpio	Oct. 24	Oct. 24	Oct. 24	Oct. 24	Oct. 24
Sagittarius	Nov. 22	Nov. 23	Nov. 23	Nov. 23	Nov. 22
Capricorn	Dec. 22	Dec. 23	Dec. 23	Dec. 23	Dec. 22

	1945	1946	1947	1948	1949
Aquarius	Jan. 20	Jan. 21	Jan. 21	Jan. 21	Jan. 20
Pisces	Feb. 19	Feb. 19	Feb. 19	Feb. 20	Feb. 19
Aries	Mar. 21	Mar. 21	Mar. 21	Mar. 21	Mar. 21
Taurus	April 20	April 21	April 21	April 20	April 20
Gemini	May 21	May 22	May 22	May 21	May 21
Cancer	June 22	June 22	June 22	June 22	June 22
Leo	July 23	July 23	July 24	July 23	July 23
Virgo	Aug. 24	Aug. 24	Aug. 24	Aug. 23	Aug. 23
Libra	Sept. 23	Sept. 24	Sept. 24	Sept. 23	Sept. 23
Scorpio	Oct. 24	Oct. 24	Oct. 24	Oct. 24	Oct. 24
Sagittarius	Nov. 23	Nov. 23	Nov. 23	Nov. 22	Nov. 23
Capricorn	Dec. 22	Dec. 22	Dec. 23	Dec. 22	Dec. 22

	1950	1951	1952	1953	1954
Aquarius	Jan. 21	Jan. 21	Jan. 21	Jan. 20	Jan. 21
Pisces	Feb. 19	Feb. 19	Feb. 20	Feb. 19	Feb. 19
Aries	Mar. 21	Mar. 21	Mar. 21	Mar. 21	Mar. 21
Taurus	April 21	April 21	April 20	April 20	April 21
Gemini	May 22	May 22	May 21	May 21	May 22
Cancer	June 22	June 22	June 21	June 22	June 22
Leo	July 23	July 24	July 23	July 23	July 23
Virgo	Aug. 24	Aug. 24	Aug. 23	Aug. 23	Aug. 24
Libra	Sept. 24	Sept. 24	Sept. 23	Sept. 23	Sept. 24
Scorpio	Oct. 24	Oct. 24	Oct. 23	Oct. 24	Oct. 24
Sagittarius	Nov. 23	Nov. 23	Nov. 22	Nov. 23	Nov. 23
Capricorn	Dec. 22	Dec. 23	Dec. 22	Dec. 22	Dec. 22

	1955	1956	1957	1958	1959
Aquarius	Jan. 21	Jan. 21	Jan. 20	Jan. 21	Jan. 21
Pisces	Feb. 19	Feb. 20	Feb. 19	Feb. 19	Feb. 19
Aries	Mar. 21	Mar. 21	Mar. 21	Mar. 21	Mar. 21
Taurus	April 21	April 20	April 20	April 21	April 21
Gemini	May 22	May 21	May 21	May 22	May 22
Cancer	June 22	June 21	June 22	June 22	June 22
Leo	July 24	July 23	July 23	July 23	July 24
Virgo	Aug. 24	Aug. 23	Aug. 23	Aug. 24	Aug. 24
Libra	Sept. 24	Sept. 23	Sept. 23	Sept. 24	Sept. 24
Scorpio	Oct. 24	Oct. 23	Oct. 24	Oct. 24	Oct. 24
Sagittarius	Nov. 23	Nov. 22	Nov. 23	Nov. 23	Nov. 23
Capricorn	Dec. 23	Dec. 22	Dec. 22	Dec. 22	Dec. 23

	1960	1961	1962	1963	1964
Aquarius	Jan. 21	Jan. 20	Jan. 21	Jan. 21	Jan. 21
Pisces	Feb. 20	Feb. 19	Feb. 19	Feb. 19	Feb. 20
Aries	Mar. 21	Mar. 21	Mar. 21	Mar. 21	Mar. 21
Taurus	April 20	April 20	April 21	April 21	April 20
Gemini	May 21	May 21	May 22	May 22	May 21
Cancer	June 21	June 22	June 22	June 22	June 21
Leo	July 23	July 23	July 23	July 24	July 23
Virgo	Aug. 23	Aug. 23	Aug. 24	Aug. 24	Aug. 23
Libra	Sept. 23	Sept. 23	Sept. 24	Sept. 24	Sept. 23
Scorpio	Oct. 23	Oct. 24	Oct. 24	Oct. 23	Oct. 23
Sagittarius	Nov. 22	Nov. 23	Nov. 23	Nov. 23	Nov. 22
Capricorn	Dec. 22	Dec. 22	Dec. 22	Dec. 23	Dec. 22

	1965	1966	1967	1968	1969
Aquarius	Jan. 20	Jan. 21	Jan. 21	Jan. 21	Jan. 20
Pisces	Feb. 19	Feb. 19	Feb. 19	Feb. 20	Feb. 19
Aries	Mar. 21	Mar. 21	Mar. 21	Mar. 21	Mar. 21
Taurus	April 20	April 21	April 21	April 20	April 20
Gemini	May 21	May 22	May 22	May 21	May 21
Cancer	June 22	June 22	June 22	June 21	June 22
Leo	July 23	July 23	July 24	July 23	July 23
Virgo	Aug. 23	Aug. 24	Aug. 24	Aug. 23	Aug. 23
Libra	Sept. 23	Sept. 23	Sept. 24	Sept. 23	Sept. 23
Scorpio	Oct. 24	Oct. 24	Oct. 24	Oct. 23	Oct. 24
Sagittarius	Nov. 23	Nov. 23	Nov. 23	Nov. 22	Nov. 22
Capricorn	Dec. 22	Dec. 22	Dec. 23	Dec. 22	Dec. 22

	1970	1971	1972	1973	1974
Aquarius	Jan. 20	Jan. 21	Jan. 21	Jan. 20	Jan. 20
Pisces	Feb. 19	Feb. 19	Feb. 20	Feb. 19	Feb. 19
Aries	Mar. 21	Mar. 21	Mar. 21	Mar. 21	Mar. 21
Taurus	April 21	April 21	April 20	April 20	April 20
Gemini	May 21	May 22	May 21	May 21	May 21
Cancer	June 22	June 22	June 21	June 22	June 22
Leo	July 23	July 24	July 23	July 23	July 23
Virgo	Aug. 24	Aug. 24	Aug. 23	Aug. 23	Aug. 24
Libra	Sept. 23	Sept. 24	Sept. 23	Sept. 23	Sept. 23
Scorpio	Oct. 24	Oct. 24	Oct. 23	Oct. 24	Oct. 24
Sagittarius	Nov. 23	Nov. 23	Nov. 22	Nov. 22	Nov. 23
Capricorn	Dec. 22	Dec. 23	Dec. 22	Dec. 22	Dec. 22

	1975	1976	1977	1978	1979
Aquarius	Jan. 21	Jan. 21	Jan. 20	Jan. 20	Jan. 21
Pisces	Feb. 19	Feb. 20	Feb. 19	Feb. 19	Feb. 19
Aries	Mar. 21	Mar. 20	Mar. 21	Mar. 21	Mar. 21
Taurus	April 21	April 20	April 20	April 20	April 21
Gemini	May 22	May 21	May 21	May 21	May 22
Cancer	June 22	June 21	June 22	June 22	June 22
Leo	July 23	July 23	July 23	July 23	July 23
Virgo	Aug. 24	Aug. 23	Aug. 23	Aug. 23	Aug. 24
Libra	Sept. 24	Sept. 23	Sept. 23	Sept. 23	Sept. 24
Scorpio	Oct. 24	Oct. 23	Oct. 24	Oct. 24	Oct. 24
Sagittarius	Nov. 23	Nov. 22	Nov. 22	Nov. 23	Nov. 23
Capricorn	Dec. 22	Dec. 22	Dec. 22	Dec. 22	Dec. 22

	1980	1981	1982	1983	1984
Aquarius	Jan. 21	Jan. 20	Jan. 20	Jan. 21	Jan. 21
Pisces	Feb. 20	Feb. 19	Feb. 19	Feb. 19	Feb. 19
Aries	Mar. 20	Mar. 21	Mar. 21	Mar. 21	Mar. 20
Taurus	April 20	April 20	April 20	April 21	April 20
Gemini	May 21	May 21	May 21	May 22	May 21
Cancer	June 21	June 21	June 22	June 22	June 21
Leo	July 23	July 23	July 23	July 23	July 23
Virgo	Aug. 23	Aug. 23	Aug. 23	Aug. 24	Aug. 23
Libra	Sept. 23	Sept. 23	Sept. 23	Sept. 24	Sept. 23
Scorpio	Oct. 23	Oct. 24	Oct. 24	Oct. 24	Oct. 23
Sagittarius	Nov. 22	Nov. 22	Nov. 23	Nov. 23	Nov. 22
Capricorn	Dec. 22	Dec. 22	Dec. 22	Dec. 22	Dec. 22

	1985	1986	1987	1988	1989
Aquarius	Jan. 20	Jan. 20	Jan. 21	Jan. 21	Jan. 20
Pisces	Feb. 19	Feb. 19	Feb. 19	Feb. 19	Feb. 19
Aries	Mar. 21	Mar. 21	Mar. 21	Mar. 20	Mar. 21
Taurus	April 20	April 20	April 21	April 20	April 20
Gemini	May 21	May 21	May 22	May 21	May 21
Cancer	June 21	June 22	June 22	June 21	June 21
Leo	July 23	July 23	July 23	July 23	July 23
Virgo	Aug. 23	Aug. 23	Aug. 24	Aug. 23	Aug. 23
Libra	Sept. 23	Sept. 23	Sept. 24	Sept. 23	Sept. 23
Scorpio	Oct. 23	Oct. 24	Oct. 24	Oct. 23	Oct. 23
Sagittarius	Nov. 22	Nov. 23	Nov. 23	Nov. 22	Nov. 22
Capricorn	Dec. 22	Dec. 22	Dec. 22	Dec. 22	Dec. 22

	1990	1991	1992	1993	1994
Aquarius	Jan. 20	Jan. 21	Jan. 21	Jan. 20	Jan. 20
Pisces	Feb. 19	Feb. 19	Feb. 19	Feb. 19	Feb. 19
Aries	Mar. 21	Mar. 21	Mar. 20	Mar. 21	Mar. 21
Taurus	April 20	April 21	April 20	April 20	April 20
Gemini	May 21	May 22	May 21	May 21	May 21
Cancer	June 22	June 22	June 21	June 21	June 22
Leo	July 23	July 23	July 23	July 23	July 23
Virgo	Aug. 23	Aug. 24	Aug. 23	Aug. 23	Aug. 23
Libra	Sept. 23	Sept. 24	Sept. 23	Sept. 23	Sept. 23
Scorpio	Oct. 24	Oct. 24	Oct. 23	Oct. 23	Oct. 24
Sagittarius	Nov. 23	Nov. 23	Nov. 22	Nov. 22	Nov. 23
Capricorn	Dec. 22	Dec. 22	Dec. 22	Dec. 22	Dec. 22

	1995	1996	1997	1998	1999
Aquarius	Jan. 21	Jan. 21	Jan. 20	Jan. 20	Jan. 21
Pisces	Feb. 19	Feb. 19	Feb. 19	Feb. 19	Feb. 19
Aries	Mar. 21	Mar. 20	Mar. 21	Mar. 21	Mar. 21
Taurus	April 21	April 20	April 20	April 20	April 21
Gemini	May 22	May 21	May 21	May 21	May 21
Cancer	June 22	June 21	June 21	June 22	June 22
Leo	July 23	July 23	July 23	July 23	July 23
Virgo	Aug. 24	Aug. 23	Aug. 23	Aug. 23	Aug. 24
Libra	Sept. 24	Sept. 23	Sept. 23	Sept. 23	Sept. 23
Scorpio	Oct. 24	Oct. 23	Oct. 23	Oct. 24	Oct. 24
Sagittarius	Nov. 23	Nov. 22	Nov. 22	Nov. 23	Nov. 23
Capricorn	Dec. 22	Dec. 22	Dec. 22	Dec. 22	Dec. 22

Appendix C.

Calorie/Carbohydrate/Protein Counter

Substitute or exchange foods that are of equal or lesser value.

	Portion	(Calories) Food Energy	Protein (in grams)	Carbohydrate (in grams)
DAIRY PRODUCTS (Cheese, Cream, Imitation Cream, Milk, Related Products)				
Cheese				
Natural				
Blue	1 oz.	100	6	1
Camembert (3 wedges per 4 oz. container)	1 wedge	115	8	0
Cheddar	1 oz.	115	7	0
Shredded	1 cup	445	28	1
Cottage (4% fat)				
Large Curd	1 cup	235	28	6
Small Curd	1 cup	220	26	6
Low Fat (2%)	1 cup	205	31	8
Low Fat (1%)	1 cup	165	28	6
Uncreamed (dry curd) Less than ½% fat	1 cup	125	25	0
Cream	1 oz.	100	2	1
Mozzarella				
Whole milk	1 oz.	90	6	1
Part skim milk	1 oz.	80	8	1
Parmesan (grated)	1 cup	455	42	4
	1 tbsp	25	2	0
	1 oz.	130	12	1
Provolone	1 oz.	100	7	1
Ricotta				
Whole milk	1 cup	428	28	7
Part skim milk	1 cup	340	28	13
Romano	1 oz.	110	9	1
Swiss	1 oz.	105	8	1

	Portion	(Calories) Food Energy	Protein (in grams)	Carbohydrate (in grams)
Pasteurized Process Cheese				
American	1 oz.	105	6	0
Swiss	1 oz.	95	7	1
American Spread	1 oz.	82	5	2
American cheese-food	1 oz.	95	6	2
Cream				
Sweet	1 cup	315	7	10
Half and Half	1 tbsp	20	0	1
Light, coffee or table	1 cup	470	6	9
	1 tbsp	30	0	1
Whipping Cream				
Light	1 cup	700	5	7
	1 tbsp	45	0	0
Heavy	1 cup	820	5	7
	1 tbsp	80	0	0
Whipped Topping	1 cup	155	2	7
	1 tbsp	10	0	0
Cream, sour	1 cup	495	7	10
	1 tbsp	25	0	1
Cream products, Imitation (with vegetable fat)				
Sweet Creamers				
Liquid (frozen)	1 cup	335	2	28
	1 tbsp	20	0	2
Powdered	1 cup	515	5	52
	1 tbsp	10	0	1
Whipped Topping				
Frozen	1 cup	240	1	17
	1 tbsp	15	0	1
Powdered (whole milk)	1 tbsp	10	0	1
Sour Dressing				
(non-fat dry milk)	1 tbsp	20	0	1

	Portion	(Calories) Food Energy	Protein (in grams)	Carbohydrate (in grams)
Milk				
Whole, 3.3% fat	1 cup	150	8	11
Lowfat (2%)	1 cup	120	8	12
Lowfat (1%)	1 cup	100	8	12
Nonfat (skim)	1 cup	85	8	12
Buttermilk	1 cup	100	8	12
Canned Milk				
Evaporated, unsweetened				
Whole milk	1 cup	340	17	25
Skim milk	1 cup	200	19	29
Condensed, unsweeted	1 cup	980	24	116
Dried Milk				
Buttermilk	1 cup	465	41	59
Nonfat instant: envelope,				
3.2 oz net weight	1 env.	325	32	47
	1 cup	245	24	35
Milk Beverages				
Chocolate milk, commercial				
regular	1 cup	210	8	26
Lowfat (2%)	1 cup	180	8	26
Lowfat (1%)	1 cup	160	8	26
Eggnog (commercial)	1 cup	340	10	34
Malted Milk				
(non-commercial)	1 cup of			
¾ oz powder	milk &			
Chocolate	¾ oz of			
	powder	235	9	29
Natural	" "	235	11	27
Shakes, thick				
Chocolate, 10.6 oz. net				
weight container	1 con.	355	9	63
Vanilla, 11 oz. net				
weight container	1 con.	350	12	56
Milk Desserts, frozen				
Ice Cream (11% fat)	½ gal.	2,155	38	254
	1 cup	270	5	32
Ice Milk (4.3% fat)	½ gal.	1,470	41	232
Sherbet (2% fat)	½ gal.	2,160	17	469
	1 cup	270	2	59

	Portion	(Calories) Food Energy	Protein (in grams)	Carbohydrate (in grams)
Milk Desserts, other				
Custard, baked	1 cup	305	14	29
Pudding				
Chocolate (home recipe)	1 cup	385	8	67
Vanilla (home recipe)	1 cup	285	9	41
Tapioca cream	1 cup	220	8	28
From mix (choc.) and milk				
Regular (cooked)	1 cup	320	9	59
Instant	1 cup	325	8	63
Yogurt				
Lowfat milk, fruit flavored				
1 container	8 oz.	230	10	42
Plain (1 container)	8 oz.	145	12	16
EGGS, *Large*				
Raw, whole	1 egg	80	6	1
Cooked				
Fried in butter	1 egg	85	5	1
Hard-boiled	1 egg	80	6	1
Poached	1 egg	80	6	1
Scrambled (milk added)				
in butter or omelet	1 egg	95	6	1
FATS, OILS, RELATED PRODUCTS				
Butter				
Regular stick, ½ cup	1 stick	815	1	0
	1 tbsp	100	0	0
	1 pat	35	0	0
Whipped ½ cup	½ cup	540	1	0
	1 tbsp	65	0	0
	1 pat	25	0	0
Fats, cooking				
Vegetable shortening	1 cup	1,770	0	0
	1 tbsp	110	0	0
Lard	1 cup	1,850	0	0
	1 tbsp	115	0	0

	Portion	(Calories) Food Energy	Protein (in grams)	Carbohydrate (in grams)
Margarine				
Regular stick	½ cup	815	1	0
	1 tbsp	100	0	0
	1 pat	35	0	0
Soft margarine 1 container	½ lb	1,635	1	0
Whipped	1 stick	545	0	0
	1 tbsp	70	0	0
Oils, salad or cooking				
Corn	1 cup	1,925	0	0
	1 tbsp	14	0	0
Olive	1 cup	1,910	0	0
	1 tbsp	120	0	0
Peanut	1 cup	1,910	0	0
	1 tbsp	120	0	0
Safflower	1 cup	1,925	0	0
	1 tbsp	120	0	0
Soybean oil, hydrogenated	1 cup	1,925	0	0
	1 tbsp	120	0	0
Soybean-cottonseed blend, hydrogenated	1 cup	1,925	0	0
	1 tbsp	120	0	0
Salad Dressings, commercial				
Blue Cheese				
Regular	1 tbsp	75	1	1
Low calorie (5 cal./tsp)	1 tbsp	15	0	1
French				
Regular	1 tbsp	65	0	3
Low calorie (5 cal./tsp)	1 tbsp	15	0	2
Italian				
Regular	1 tbsp	85	0	1
Low calorie (2 cal./tsp)	1 tbsp	6	0	0
Mayonnaise	1 tbsp	100	0	0
Mayonnaise type				
Regular	1 tbsp	65	0	2
Low calorie (8 cal./tsp)	1 tbsp	24	0	2
Tartar sauce, regular	1 tbsp	75	0	1
Thousand Island				
Regular	1 tbsp	80	0	2
Low calorie (10 cal./tsp)	1 tbsp	30	0	2

	Portion	(Calories) Food Energy	Protein (in grams)	Carbohydrate (in grams)

FISH, SHELLFISH, MEAT, POULTRY; RELATED PRODUCTS

Fish and shellfish

	Portion	Food Energy	Protein	Carbohydrate
Bluefish, baked with butter or margarine	3 oz.	135	22	0
Clams				
Raw, meat only	3 oz.	65	11	2
Canned, solids and liquid	3 oz.	45	7	2
Crabmeat (white or king) canned	1 cup	135	24	1
Fishsticks, breaded, cooked, Frozen, 1 fishstick	1 oz.	50	5	2
Haddock, breaded, fried	3 oz.	140	17	5
Ocean perch, breaded, fried	1 fillet	195	16	6
Oysters, raw, meat only	1 cup	160	20	8
Salmon, pink, canned, solids and liquid	3 oz.	120	17	0
Sardines, Atlantic, in oil, drained	3 oz.	175	20	0
Scallops, frozen, breaded, fried, reheated	6	175	16	9
Shad, baked with butter or margarine, bacon	3 oz.	170	20	0
Shrimp				
Canned meat	3 oz.	100	21	1
French fried	3 oz.	190	17	9
Tuna, canned in oil, drained	3 oz.	170	24	0
Tuna Salad	1 cup	350	30	7

Meat and Meat Products

	Portion	Food Energy	Protein	Carbohydrate
Bacon, broiled or fried, crisp	2 slices	85	4	0
Beef, cooked				
Lean and fat	3 oz.	245	23	0
Lean only	2.5 oz.	140	22	0
Ground beef, broiled				
Lean with 10% fat	3 oz.	185	23	0
Lean with 21% fat	2.9 Oz.	235	20	0

	Portion	(Calories) Food Energy	Protein (in grams)	Carbohydrate (in grams)
Roast, oven cooked, no liquid added				
Lean and fat	3 oz.	375	17	0
Lean only	1.8 oz.	125	14	0
Steak, relatively fat, Sirloin, broiled				
Lean and fat	3 oz.	330	20	0
Lean only	2 oz.	115	18	0
Relatively lean round, braised				
Lean and fat	3 oz.	220	24	0
Lean only	2.4 oz.	130	21	0
Beef, canned				
Corned beef	3 oz.	185	22	0
Corned beef hash	1 cup	400	19	24
Beef, dried, chipped	2½ oz.	145	24	0
Beef and vegetable stew	1 cup	220	16	15
Beef pot pie (home recipe) baked 9" pie	1 piece	515	21	39
Chili con carne with beans Canned	1 cup	340	19	31
Chop suey with beef and pork (home recipe)	1 cup	300	26	13
Heart, beef, lean, braised	3 oz.	160	27	1
Lamb, cooked				
Chop, rib, lean and fat	3.1 oz.	360	18	0
Lean only	2 oz.	120	16	0
Leg of Lamb, roasted				
Lean and fat	3 oz.	235	22	0
Lean only	2.5 oz.	130	20	0
Shoulder, roasted				
Lean and fat	3 oz.	285	18	0
Lean only	2.3 oz.	130	17	0
Liver, beef, fried	3 oz.	195	22	5
Pork, cured, cooked, ham, light cure, lean and fat, roasted	3 oz.	245	18	0
Luncheon meat				
Boiled ham, slice	1 oz.	65	5	0
Canned, spiced or unspiced	1 slice	175	9	1
Pork, fresh cooked chop, loin				
Lean and fat	2.7 oz.	305	19	0
Lean only	2 oz.	150	17	0

	Portion	(Calories) Food Energy	Protein (in grams)	Carbohydrate (in grams)
Pork roast, oven cooked, no liquid added				
Lean and fat	3 oz.	310	21	0
Lean only	2.4 oz.	175	20	0
Pork shoulder cut, simmered				
Lean and fat	3 oz.	320	20	0
Lean only	2.2 oz.	135	18	0
Sausages				
Bologna	1 slice	85	3	0
Brown and serve, browned	1 link	70	3	0
Deviled ham, canned	1 tbsp	45	2	0
Frankfurter, cooked	1 frank	170	7	1
Meat, potted (beef, chicken, turkey) canned	1 tbsp	30	2	0
Pork link, cooked	1 link	60	2	0
Salami				
Dry type	1 slice	45	2	0
Cooked type	1 slice	90	5	0
Vienna sausage				
Canned	1	40	2	0
Veal, medium fat, cooked, bone removed				
Cutlet	3 oz.	185	23	0
Rib	3 oz.	230	23	0
Poultry and poultry products				
Chicken, cooked				
Breast, fried, deboned	2.8 oz.	160	26	1
Drumstick, fried deboned	1.3 oz.	90	12	0
Half broiler, broiled, deboned	6.2 oz.	240	42	0
Chicken, canned, boneless	3 oz.	170	18	0
Chicken a la king, cooked (home recipe)	1 cup	470	27	12
Chicken and noodles, cooked (home recipe)	1 cup	365	22	26
Chicken chow mein				
Canned	1 cup	95	7	18
Home recipe	1 cup	255	31	10

	Portion	(Calories) Food Energy	Protein (in grams)	Carbohydrate (in grams)
Chicken pot pie, home recipe, baked	1 piece	545	23	42
Turkey, roasted, skinless				
Dark meat	4 pieces	175	26	0
Light meat	2 pieces	150	28	0

FRUITS AND FRUIT PRODUCTS

	Portion	(Calories) Food Energy	Protein (in grams)	Carbohydrate (in grams)
Apples, raw, unpeeled, without cores				
2¾" diameter	1 apple	80	0	20
3½" diameter	1 apple	125	0	31
Applejuice, bottled or canned	1 cup	120	0	30
Applesauce, canned				
Sweetened	1 cup	230	1	61
Unsweetened	1 cup	100	0	26
Apricots				
Raw, without pits	3	55	1	14
Canned in heavy syrup	1 cup	220	2	57
Dried, uncooked	1 cup	340	7	86
Cooked, unsweetened, fruit and liquid	1 cup	215	4	54
Apricot nectar, canned	1 cup	145	1	37
Avocados, raw whole with skin and seed, 3¼" diam.	1	380	4	27
Banana, without peel	1	100	1	26
Blackberries, raw	1 cup	85	2	19
Blueberries, raw	1 cup	90	1	22
Cherries				
Sour, red, canned, water packed	1 cup	105	2	26
Sweet, raw, without pits and stems	10	45	1	12
Cranberry juice cocktail, bottled, sweetened	1 cup	165	0	42
Cranberry sauce, sweetened, canned	1 cup	405	0	104
Dates				
Whole	10 dates	220	2	58
Chopped	1 cup	490	4	130

	Portion	(Calories) Food Energy	Protein (in grams)	Carbohydrate (in grams)
Fruit cocktail, canned, in heavy syrup	1 cup	195	1	50
Grapefruit 3¾″ diameter,				
pink or red	½	50	1	13
white	½	45	1	12
Canned sections with syrup	1 cup	180	2	45
Juice				
Raw, pink, red or white	1 cup	95	1	23
Canned white				
Unsweetened	1 cup	100	1	24
Sweetened	1 cup	135	1	32
Frozen concentrate, unsweetened				
Undiluted, 6 fl. oz. can	1 can	300	4	72
Diluted	1 cup	100	1	24
Grapes, raw				
Seedless	10	35	0	9
Grape juice				
Canned or bottled	1 cup	165	1	42
Frozen, concentrate, sweetened Undiluted, 6 fl. oz.				
can	1 can	395	1	100
Diluted	1 cup	135	1	33
Grape drink, canned	1 cup	135	0	35
Lemon				
raw	1 lemon	20	1	6
juice				
Raw	1 cup	60	1	20
Canned or bottled, unsweetened, frozen, 6 fl. oz. can	1 can	40	1	13
Lemonade concentrate frozen				
Undiluted, 6 fl. oz. can	1 can	425	0	112
Diluted	1 cup	105	0	28
Limeade concentrate, frozen				
Undiluted, 6 fl. oz. can	1 can	410	0	108
Diluted	1 cup	100	0	27
Lime juice				
Raw	1 cup	65	1	22

	Portion	(Calories) Food Energy	Protein (in grams)	Carbohydrate (in grams)
Canned, unsweetened	1 cup	65	1	22
Cantaloupe, 5″ diameter	½ melon	80	2	20
Honeydew melon, 6½″ diameter	1/10	50	1	11
Oranges, raw	1	65	1	16
Sections	1 cup	90	2	22
Orange juice				
raw, all varieties	1 cup	110	2	26
canned, unsweetened	1 cup	120	2	28
Frozen, concentrate				
Undiluted, 6 fl. oz. can	1 can	360	5	87
Diluted	1 cup	120	2	29
Papayas, raw	1 cup	55	1	14
Peaches				
raw				
whole, peeled, 2½″ diameter	1 peach	40	1	10
canned, solids and liquid	1 cup	65	1	16
Syrup pack	1 cup	200	1	51
Water pack	1 cup	75	1	20
Frozen, sliced, sweetened,				
10 oz.	10 oz.	250	1	64
	1 cup	220	1	57
Pears				
Raw, Bartlett, 2½″ diameter	1 pear	100	1	25
Canned, solids and liquid,				
syrup pack	1 cup	195	1	50
Pineapple				
Raw, diced	1 cup	80	1	21
Canned, heavy syrup, solids				
and liquid, crushed chunks,				
tidbits	1 cup	190	1	49
Pineapple juice				
Unsweetened, canned	1 cup	140	1	34
Plums				
raw, 2⅛″ diameter	1 plum	30	0	8
Prune-type, 1½″ diameter	1 plum	20	0	6
Canned, heavy syrup	1 cup	215	1	56
Prunes				
dried, uncooked	4 prunes	110	1	29

	Portion	(Calories) Food Energy	Protein (in grams)	Carbohydrate (in grams)
Cooked, unsweetened, fruit and liquid	1 cup	225	2	67
Prune juice, canned or bottled	1 cup	195	1	49
Raisins, seedless	1 cup	420	4	112
Raspberries				
red, raw	1 cup	70	1	17
Frozen, sweetened, 10 oz. container	1	280	2	70
Rhubarb, cooked, added sugar				
Raw	1 cup	380	1	97
Frozen, sweetened	1 cup	385	1	98
Strawberries				
Raw, whole	1 cup	55	1	13
Frozen, sweetened, sliced, 10 oz. container	1	310	1	79
Tangerine, raw, 2⅜" diameter	1	40	1	10
Tangerine juice, canned, sweetened	1 cup	125	1	30
Watermelon, raw	1 wedge	110	2	27

GRAIN PRODUCTS

	Portion	(Calories) Food Energy	Protein (in grams)	Carbohydrate (in grams)
Bagel, 3" diameter	1 bagel	165	6	28
Barley, uncooked	1 cup	700	16	158
Biscuits, baking powder				
Home recipe	1 biscuit	105	2	13
From mix	1 biscuit	90	2	15
Breadcrumbs, dry, grated	1 cup	390	13	73
Breads				
Cracked wheat, 1 lb. loaf	1 loaf	1,195	39	236
	1 slice	65	2	13
French or Vienna				
French	1 slice	100	3	19
Vienna	1 slice	75	2	14
Italian	1 loaf	1,250	41	256
	1 slice	85	3	17
Raisin bread	1 loaf	1,190	30	243
	1 slice	65	2	13

	Portion	(Calories) Food Energy	Protein (in grams)	Carbohydrate (in grams)
Rye bread				
Light	1 loaf	1,100	41	236
	1 slice	60	2	13
Pumpernickel	1 loaf	1,115	41	241
	1 slice	80	3	17
White bread, enriched	1 loaf	1,225	39	229
	1 slice	70	2	13
Whole wheat bread, 1 lb.	1 loaf	1,095	41	224
	1 slice	65	3	14

Breakfast cereals

Hot type, cooked

	Portion	(Calories) Food Energy	Protein (in grams)	Carbohydrate (in grams)
Corn (hominy) grits	1 cup	125	3	27
Farina, quick cooking	1 cup	105	3	22
Oatmeal or rolled oats	1 cup	130	5	23
Wheat, rolled	1 cup	180	5	41
Wheat, whole-meal	1 cup	110	4	23

Ready-to-eat

	Portion	(Calories) Food Energy	Protein (in grams)	Carbohydrate (in grams)
Bran flakes	1 cup	105	4	28
Bran flakes with raisins, added sugar	1 cup	145	4	40
Corn flakes	1 cup	95	2	21
Sugar coated	1 cup	155	2	37
Corn, puffed, plain	1 cup	80	2	16
Oats, puffed, added sugar	1 cup	100	3	19
Rice, puffed	1 cup	60	1	13
Wheat flakes	1 cup	105	3	24
Wheat, puffed	1 cup	55	2	12
Wheat, shredded, plain	1 biscuit or ½ cup spoon-size	90	2	20
Wheat germ, w/o salt & sugar	1 tbsp.	25	2	3
Buckwheat flour	1 cup	340	6	78

Cakes made from cake mixes with enriched flour

	Portion	(Calories) Food Energy	Protein (in grams)	Carbohydrate (in grams)
Angel food	1 cake	1,645	36	377
	1 piece	135	3	32
Coffee cake	1 cake	1,385	27	225
	1 piece	230	5	38

	Portion	(Calories) Food Energy	Protein (in grams)	Carbohydrate (in grams)
Cupcakes, 2½″ diameter				
without icing	1	90	1	14
With chocolate icing	1	130	2	21
Devil's food with chocolate icing				
Whole, 2-layer cake	1 cake	3,755	49	645
	1 piece	235	3	40
	1	120	2	20
Gingerbread				
Whole cake, 8″ sq.	1 cake	1,575	18	291
	1 piece	175	2	32
White, 2 layer cake with chocolate icing	1 cake	3,735	45	638
	1 piece	250	3	45
Yellow, 2 layer cake with chocolate icing	1 cake	4,000	44	716
	1 piece	235	3	40

Cakes made from home recipes using enriched flour

	Portion	(Calories) Food Energy	Protein (in grams)	Carbohydrate (in grams)
Boston cream pie with custard filling	1 cake	2,490	41	412
	1 piece	210	3	34
Fruitcake, dark				
Loaf, 1 lb.	1 loaf	1,720	22	271
	1 slice	55	1	9
Plain sheet cake				
Without icing	1 cake	2,830	35	434
	1 piece	315	4	48
With icing	1 cake	4,020	37	694
	1 piece	445	4	77
Pound cake	1 loaf	2,725	31	273
	1 slice	160	2	16
Sponge cake	1 cake	2,345	60	427
	1 piece	195	5	36

Cookies made with enriched flour

	Portion	(Calories) Food Energy	Protein (in grams)	Carbohydrate (in grams)
Brownies with nuts				
Home prepared	1	95	1	10
Commercial	1	85	1	13
Chocolate chip				
Commercial, 2¼″ diameter	4 cookies	200	2	29
Home recipe, 2⅓″ diameter	4 cookies	205	2	24

	Portion	(Calories) Food Energy	Protein (in grams)	Carbohydrate (in grams)
Fig bars, square	4 cookies	200	2	42
Gingersnaps, 2″ diameter	4 cookies	90	2	22
Macaroons, 2¾″ diameter	2 cookies	180	2	25
Oatmeal with raisins, 2⅝″ dia.	4 cookies	235	3	38
Plain, prepared from commercial dough, 2½″ diameter	4 cookies	240	2	31
Sandwich type, chocolate or vanilla, 1¾″ diameter	4 cookies	200	2	28
Vanilla wafers, 1¾″ diameter	10	185	2	30

Cornmeal

Whole ground	1 cup	435	11	90
Degermed, enriched				
Dry form	1 cup	500	11	108
Cooked	1 cup	120	3	26

Crackers

graham, plain	2	55	1	10
Rye wafers	2	45	2	10
Saltines	4	50	1	8

Danish pastry, plain 12 oz.	1 ring	1,435	25	155

Donuts

Cake type, plain	1	100	1	13
Glazed	1	205	3	22

Macaroni, enriched, cooked

Cold	1 cup	115	4	24
Hot	1 cup	155	5	32

Macaroni and cheese, enriched

Canned	1 cup	230	9	26
Home recipe, served hot	1 cup	430	17	40

Muffins, enriched flour

Home recipe, Blueberry, 2⅜″ dia.	1 muffin	110	3	17
Bran	1 muffin	105	3	17
Corn	1 muffin	125	3	19
Plain	1 muffin	120	3	17

	Portion	(Calories) Food Energy	Protein (in grams)	Carbohydrate (in grams)
From mix, egg, milk				
Corn, 2⅜″ diameter	1 muffin	130	3	20
Noodles, (egg)				
enriched				
Cooked	1 cup	200	7	37
Noodles, chow mein, canned	1 cup	220	6	26
Pancakes, 4″ diameter				
Buckwheat, made from mix	1 cake	55	2	6
Plain, made from home recipe	1 cake	60	2	9
Pies, piecrust 9″ diameter				
Apple, whole	1 pie	2,420	21	360
	1 piece	345	3	51
Banana cream	1 pie	2,010	41	279
	1 piece	285	6	40
Blueberry	1 pie	2,285	23	330
	1 piece	325	3	47
Cherry	1 pie	2,465	25	363
	1 piece	350	4	52
Custard	1 pie	1,985	56	213
	1 piece	285	8	30
Lemon meringue	1 pie	2,140	31	317
	1 piece	305	4	45
Mince	1 pie	2,560	24	389
	1 piece	365	3	56
Peach	1 pie	2,410	24	361
	1 piece	345	3	52
Pecan	1 pie	3,450	42	423
	1 piece	495	6	61
Pumpkin	1 pie	1,920	36	223
	1 piece	275	5	32
Piecrust, home baked, 9″	1 shell	900	11	79
Pizza, cheese, baked	1 slice	145	6	22
Popcorn, popped				
Plain	1 cup	25	1	5
With oil added	1 cup	40	1	5
Sugar coated	1 cup	135	2	30

	Portion	(Calories) Food Energy	Protein (in grams)	Carbohydrate (in grams)
Pretzels, made with enriched flour				
Dutch, twisted	1	60	2	12
Thin, twisted	10	235	6	46
Stick, 2¼″ long	10	10	0	2
Rice, white, enriched				
Instant, ready-to-serve, hot	1 cup	180	4	40
Long grain, raw	1 cup	670	12	149
Cooked, served hot	1 cup	225	4	50
Parboiled				
Raw	1 cup	685	14	150
Cooked, served hot	1 cup	185	4	41
Rolls, enriched, commercial				
Brown and serve, 1 oz.	1 roll	85	2	14
Pan, 2½″ diameter	1 roll	85	2	15
Frankfurter and hamburger	1 roll	120	3	21
Hard, 3¾″ diameter	1 roll	155	5	30
Hoagie or submarine	1 roll	390	12	75
Spaghetti, enriched, cooked				
Firm, served hot	1 cup	190	7	39
Tender, served hot	1 cup	155	5	32
Spaghetti, enriched, in tomato sauce with cheese				
Home recipe	1 cup	260	9	37
Canned	1 cup	190	6	39
Spaghetti with meatballs and tomato sauce				
Home recipe	1 cup	330	19	39
Canned	1 cup	260	12	29
Toaster pastries	1 pastry	200	3	36
Waffles, made with enriched flour, 7″ diameter				
Home recipe	1 waffle	210	7	28
From mix, egg and milk added	1 waffle	205	7	27
Wheat flours				
All purpose or family flour, enriched				
Sifted	1 cup	420	12	88
Unsifted	1 cup	455	13	95

	Portion	(Calories) Food Energy	Protein (in grams)	Carbohydrate (in grams)
Cake or pastry flour, enriched				
Sifted	1 cup	350	7	76
Self-rising, enriched, unsifted	1 cup	440	12	93
Whole wheat	1 cup	400	16	85

LEGUMES (Dry), NUTS, SEEDS; RELATED PRODUCTS

	Portion	(Calories) Food Energy	Protein (in grams)	Carbohydrate (in grams)
Almonds, chopped	1 cup	775	24	25
Slivered	1 cup	690	21	22
Beans, dry				
Great Northern navy, and others				
Cooked, drained	1 cup	215	15	39
Canned, solids and liquid				
White with frankfurters	1 cup	365	19	32
Pork and tomato sauce	1 cup	310	16	48
Red kidney	1 cup	230	15	42
Lima, cooked, drained	1 cup	260	16	49
Blackeye peas, dry, cooked	1 cup	190	13	35
Brazil nuts	1 oz.	185	4	3
Cashew nuts, roasted in oil	1 cup	785	24	41
Coconut meat, fresh, 2″ × 2″ × ½″	1 piece	155	2	4
Shredded or grated	1 cup	275	3	8
Filberts (hazelnuts)				
Chopped	1 cup	730	14	19
Lentils, whole, cooked	1 cup	210	16	39
Peanuts, roasted in oil, salted	1 cup	840	37	27
Peanut butter	1 tbsp.	95	4	3
Peas, split, dry cooked	1 cup	230	16	42
Pecans, chopped	1 cup	810	11	17
Sunflower seeds, dry, hulled	1 cup	810	35	29
Walnuts, black:				
Chopped or broken	1 cup	785	26	19

	Portion	(Calories) Food Energy	Protein (in grams)	Carbohydrate (in grams)
Cake icings				
Boiled white				
Plain	1 cup	295	1	75
With coconut	1 cup	605	3	124
Uncooked				
Chocolate made with milk				
and butter	1 cup	1,035	9	185
Creamy fudge from mix and				
water	1 cup	830	7	183
White	1 cup	1,200	2	260
Candy				
Caramels, plain, milk, chocolate	1 oz.	145	2	16
Semi-sweet	1 cup	860	7	97
Chocolate-coated peanuts	1 oz.	160	5	11
Fondant, uncoated, mints,				
candy, corn, other	1 oz.	105	0	25
Fudge, chocolate, plain	1 oz.	115	1	21
Gum drops	1 oz.	100	0	25
Marshmallows	1 oz.	90	1	23
Chocolate-flavored beverage powders (about 4 heaping tsp. per oz.)				
With non-fat dry milk	1 oz.	100	5	20
Without milk	1 oz.	100	1	25
Honey, strained or extracted	1 tbsp.	65	0	17
Jams and preserves	1 tbsp.	55	0	14
Jellies	1 tbsp.	50	0	13
Syrups				
Chocolate-flavored syrup or topping				
Thin type	1 fl. oz. or 2 tbsp.	90	1	24
Fudge type	1 fl. oz. or 2 tbsp.	125	2	20
Molasses, cane				
Light	1 tbsp.	50	0	13
Blackstrap	1 tbsp.	45	0	11
Table blends, corn, light				
and dark	1 tbsp.	60	0	15

	Portion	(Calories) Food Energy	Protein (in grams)	Carbohydrate (in grams)
Sugars				
Brown, pressed down	1 cup	820	0	212
White, granulated	1 cup	770	0	199
	1 tbsp.	45	0	12
Powdered, sifted	1 cup	385	0	100

VEGETABLES, Green, Yellow, Others

	Portion	(Calories) Food Energy	Protein (in grams)	Carbohydrate (in grams)
Asparagus, green, cooked, drained, cuts and tips, 1½″ to 2″ lengths				
Raw	1 cup	30	3	5
Frozen	1 cup	40	6	6
Spears, ½″ diameter				
Raw	4 spears	10	1	2
Frozen, canned	4 spears	15	2	2
Beans				
Lima, frozen, cooked, drained				
Fordhooks	1 cup	170	10	32
Baby limas	1 cup	210	13	40
Snap, green, cooked, drained				
Raw, cuts and French style	1 cup	30	2	7
Frozen, cuts	1 cup	35	2	8
French style	1 cup	35	2	8
Canned, drained solids, cuts	1 cup	30	2	7
Yellow or wax, cooked, drained				
Raw, cuts and French style	1 cup	30	2	6
Frozen, cuts	1 cup	35	2	8
Bean sprouts				
Raw	1 cup	35	4	7
Cooked, drained	1 cup	35	4	7
Beets, cooked, drained, peeled				
Whole fresh beets, 2″ diameter	2 beets	30	1	7
Diced or sliced fresh	1 cup	55	2	12
Canned, drained solids				
Whole beets, diced or sliced	1 cup	62	2	15
Beet greens, leaves and stems, cooked, drained	1 cup	25	2	5
Blackeye peas, cooked and drained				
Raw	1 cup	180	13	30
Frozen	1 cup	220	15	40

	Portion	(Calories) Food Energy	Protein (in grams)	Carbohydrate (in grams)
Broccoli, cooked, drained				
Raw, stalk, medium size	1 stalk	45	6	8
Frozen, stalk 4½″ to 5″ long	1 stalk	10	1	1
Chopped	1 cup	50	5	9
Brussels sprouts, cooked, drained				
Raw	1 cup	55	7	10
Frozen	1 cup	50	5	10
Cabbage				
Raw, shredded or sliced	1 cup	18	1	5
Carrots				
Raw, scraped	1	30	1	7
Grated	1 cup	45	1	11
Cooked, drained	1 cup	50	1	11
Canned				
Sliced, drained solids	1 cup	45	1	10
Strained or junior (baby food)	1 oz.	10	0	2
Cauliflower				
Raw, chopped	1 cup	31	3	6
Cooked, drained				
Fresh (flower buds)	1 cup	30	3	5
Frozen (flowerets)	1 cup	30	3	6
Celery				
Pascal type, raw	1 stalk	5	0	2
Pieces, diced	1 cup	20	1	5
Collards				
Cooked, drained				
Fresh	1 cup	65	7	10
Frozen (chopped)	1 cup	50	5	10
Corn, sweet				
Cooked, drained				
Fresh	1 ear	70	2	16
Frozen, 5″ long	1 ear	120	4	27
Kernels	1 cup	130	5	31
Canned				
Cream style	1 cup	210	5	51
Whole kernel, vacuum pack	1 cup	175	5	43
Wet pack, drained solids	1 cup	140	4	33

	Portion	(Calories) Food Energy	Protein (in grams)	Carbohydrate (in grams)
Cucumber slices				
with peel	6 large or 8 small	5	0	1
without peel	6½ large or 9 small	5	0	1
Dandelion greens, cooked, drained	1 cup	35	2	7
Endive, curly, raw, (including escarole)	1 cup	10	1	2
Kale, cooked and drained				
Raw	1 cup	45	5	7
Frozen, leaf style	1 cup	40	4	7
Lettuce, raw				
Iceberg, 6″ diameter	1 head	70	5	16
Pieces, chopped or shredded	1 cup	5	0	2
Mushrooms, raw, sliced or chopped	1 cup	20	2	3
Mustard greens, cooked, drained	1 cup	30	3	6
Okra pods, cooked	10 pods	30	2	6
Onions				
Raw, chopped	1 cup	65	3	15
Raw, sliced	1 cup	45	2	10
Cooked, whole or sliced, drained	1 cup	60	3	14
Parsley, raw, chopped	1 tbsp.	0	0	0
Parsnips, cooked	1 cup	100	2	23
Peas, green				
Canned, whole, drained solids	1 cup	150	8	29
Strained (baby food)	1 oz.	15	1	3
Frozen, cooked, drained	1 cup	110	8	19

	Portion	(Calories) Food Energy	Protein (in grams)	Carbohydrate (in grams)
Peppers				
Hot, red, without seeds, dried	1 tsp.	5	0	1
Sweet, stem and seeds removed				
or cooked and drained	1 pod	15	1	4
Potatoes, cooked				
Baked, peeled after baking	1 potato	156	4	33
Boiled, peeled after boiling	1	105	3	23
French fried, raw	1 potato	135	2	18
Frozen, oven heated	10 strips	110	2	17
Hash brown, prepared from				
frozen	1 cup	345	3	45
Mashed, prepared from raw,				
Milk added	1 cup	135	4	27
Milk and butter added	1 cup	195	4	26
Potato chips	10 chips	115	1	10
Potato salad	1 cup	250	7	41
Pumpkin, canned	1 cup	80	2	19
Radishes, raw	4	5	0	1
Sauerkraut, canned, solids and liquid	1 cup	40	2	9
Spinach				
Raw, chopped	1 cup	15	2	2
Cooked, drained				
Raw	1 cup	40	5	6
Frozen, chopped or leaf	1 cup	45	6	7
Squash, cooked				
Summer (all varieties), diced,				
drained	1 cup	30	2	7
Winter (all varieties), baked				
and mashed	1 cup	130	4	32
Sweet potatoes				
Cooked raw, baked in skin,				
peeled	1	160	2	37
Boiled in skin, peeled	1	170	3	40
Candied (2½″ × 2″ piece)	1 piece	175	1	36

	Portion	(Calories) Food Energy	Protein (in grams)	Carbohydrate (in grams)
Canned				
Solid pack, mashed	1 cup	275	5	63
Vacuum pack	1 piece	45	1	10
Tomatoes				
Raw, 2⅗" diameter	1 tomato	25	1	6
Canned, solids and liquid	1 cup	50	2	10
Tomato catsup	1 cup	290	5	69
	1 tbsp.	15	0	4
Tomato juice, canned	1 cup	45	2	10
	1 glass (6 fl. oz.)	35	2	8
Turnips, cooked				
Diced	1 cup	35	1	8
Turnip greens, cooked drained				
Raw	1 cup	30	3	5
Frozen, chopped	1 cup	40	4	6
Vegetables, mixed, frozen, cooked	1 cup	115	6	24

MISCELLANEOUS ITEMS

	Portion	(Calories) Food Energy	Protein (in grams)	Carbohydrate (in grams)
Baking powder	1 tsp.	5	0	1
Low sodium	1 tsp.	5	0	2
Barbecue sauce	1 cup	230	4	20
Beverages, alcoholic				
Beer	12 fl. oz.	150	1	14
Gin, rum vodka, whiskey				
80-proof	1½ fl. oz.	95	0	0
86-proof	1½ fl. oz.	105	0	0
90-proof	1½ fl. oz.	110	0	0
Wines				
Dessert	3½ fl. oz.	140	0	8
Table	3½ fl. oz.	85	0	4
Beverages, carbonated, sweetened, non-alcoholic				
Carbonated water	12 fl. oz.	115	0	29

	Portion	(Calories) Food Energy	Protein (in grams)	Carbohydrate (in grams)
Cola type	12 fl. oz.	145	0	37
Fruit-flavored sodas and Tom Collins mixer	12 fl. oz.	170	0	45
Ginger ale	12 fl. oz.	115	0	29
Root beer	12 fl. oz.	150	0	39

Chocolate

	Portion	(Calories) Food Energy	Protein (in grams)	Carbohydrate (in grams)
Bitter or baking	1 oz.	145	3	8

Gelatin, dry

	Portion	(Calories) Food Energy	Protein (in grams)	Carbohydrate (in grams)
	1, 7-g. env.	25	6	0
Gelatin dessert prepared with powder and water	1 cup	140	4	34

Mustard, prepared, yellow

	Portion	(Calories) Food Energy	Protein (in grams)	Carbohydrate (in grams)
	1 tsp.	5	0	0

Olives, pickled, canned, green

	Portion	(Calories) Food Energy	Protein (in grams)	Carbohydrate (in grams)
	4 med.	15	0	0

Pickles, cucumber

	Portion	(Calories) Food Energy	Protein (in grams)	Carbohydrate (in grams)
Dill, medium, whole	1 pickle	5	0	1
Fresh, pack, slices	2 slices	10	0	3
Sweet, gherkin, small	1 pickle	20	0	5

Relish, finely chopped, sweet

	Portion	(Calories) Food Energy	Protein (in grams)	Carbohydrate (in grams)
	1 tbsp.	20	0	5

Popsicle, 3 fl. oz.

	Portion	(Calories) Food Energy	Protein (in grams)	Carbohydrate (in grams)
	1 pop.	70	0	18

Soups

Canned, condensed
Prepared with milk

	Portion	(Calories) Food Energy	Protein (in grams)	Carbohydrate (in grams)
Cream of chicken	1 cup	180	7	15
Cream of mushroom	1 cup	215	7	16
Tomato	1 cup	175	7	23

Prepared with water

	Portion	(Calories) Food Energy	Protein (in grams)	Carbohydrate (in grams)
Bean with pork	1 cup	170	8	22
Beef broth, bouillon, consommé	1 cup	30	5	3
Beef noodle	1 cup	65	4	7
Clam chowder, Manhattan type, without milk, with tomatoes	1 cup	80	2	12
Cream of chicken	1 cup	95	3	8

	Portion	(Calories) Food Energy	Protein (in grams)	Carbohydrate (in grams)
Cream of mushroom	1 cup	135	2	10
Minestrone	1 cup	105	5	14
Split pea	1 cup	145	9	21
Tomato	1 cup	90	2	16
Vegetable beef	1 cup	80	5	10
Vegetarian	1 cup	80	2	13
Dehydrated				
Bouillon cube	1 cube	5	1	0
Mixes				
Unprepared				
Onion	1½ oz. pkg.	150	6	23
Prepared with water				
Chicken noodle	1 cup	55	2	8
Onion	1 cup	35	1	6
Tomato vegetable with noodles	1 cup	65	1	12
Vinegar, cider	1 tbsp.	0	0	1
White sauce, medium, with enriched flour	1 cup	405	10	22
Yeast				
Baker's, dry, active	1 pkg.	20	3	3
Brewer's dry	1 tbsp.	25	3	3

Source: U.S. Department of Agriculture.

Air Signs:
These signs express themselves mentally. (Gemini, Libra, and Aquarius.)

Astrology:
The study of planetary patterns and how they affect the human condition.

Astronomy:
The science of planetary patterns.

Cardinal Signs:
These are the changeable signs governing the beginning of each season. (Aries, Cancer, Libra, and Capricorn.)

Common Signs:
These are the planning signs. (Gemini, Virgo, Sagittarius, and Pisces.)

Cusp:
The beginning of any new sign or house.

Earth Signs:
These signs express themselves in a practical manner. (Taurus, Virgo, and Capricorn.)

Fire Signs:
These are the action signs. (Aries, Leo, and Sagittarius.)

Fixed Signs:
These signs are constant, steady, and reliable. (Taurus, Leo, Scorpio, and Aquarius.)

Houses:
These designate twelve distinct areas of life on the astrological wheel.

Horoscope:
This is a map representing the heavens at the time of birth.

Transit:
When a planet, sun, or moon passes over any point in the horoscope.

Water Signs:
These signs express themselves emotionally. (Cancer, Scorpio, and Pisces.)

Bibliography

Astarte. *Astrology Made Easy*. North Hollywood, California: Wilshire Book Company, 1977.

Goodman, Linda. *Sun Signs*. New York: Bantam Books, 1968.

Hand, Robert. *Planets in Transit*. Rockport, Massachusetts: Para Research, Inc., 1976.

——————— *Planets in Youth*. Rockport, Massachusetts: Para Research, Inc., 1977.

Hickey, Isabel. *Astrology*. Watertown, Massachusetts: Fellowship House, 1979.

Holmes, Tiffany. *Woman's Astrology*. New York: E. P. Dutton and Co., 1977.

Leek, Sybil. *The Astrological Guide to Beauty*. New York: Popular Library, 1973.

Leo, Alan. *Astrology For All*. New York: Astrologer's Library, 1978.

——————— *Dictionary of Astrology*. New York: Astrologer's Library, 1978.

——————— *How to Judge a Nativity*. New York: Astrologer's Library, 1978.

——————— *The Key to Your Own Nativity*. New York: Astrologer's Library, 1978.

Llewellyn, George. *The New A to Z Horoscope Maker and Delineator*. St. Paul, Minnesota: Llewellyn Publications, 1981.

Michelsen, Neil F. *The American Ephermeris for the 20th Century: 1900-2000 at Midnight.* Rockport, Massachusetts: Para Research, Inc., 1980.

Parker, Else. *Astrology.* North Hollywood, California: Newcastle Publishing Co., Inc., 1977.

Pelletier, Robert. *Planets in Aspect.* Rockport, Massachusetts: Para Research, Inc., 1974.

Rathgeb, Marlene Masini. *Success Signs.* New York: St. Martin's Press, 1981.

Sakoian, Frances and Acker, Louis. *The Astrologer's Handbook.* New York: Harper and Row, 1973.

_____. *Predictive Astrology.* New York: Harper and Row, 1977.

Stern, Judith and Denberg, S. *The Fast Food Diet.* Englewood Cliffs, New Jersey: Prentice-Hall, Inc., 1980.

U.S. Department of Agriculture, Agricultural Research Service. *Nutritive Value of Foods.* Washignton, D.C.: Government Printing Office, 1977.

Zolar. *Zolar's Horoscope and Lucky Number Dream Book.* Prentice Books, Inc., 1980.

Suggested Reading

The Stress FoodBook
The Natural Way to Fight Stress
by Margaret C. Dean, M.S., R.D.
illustrated by Loel Barr

Today everyone lives under stress. It is a constant factor in our lives, and some stress is good for you. It motivates you to act. But when there is too much stress, or it lasts too long, it affects your health.

But now there is **THE STRESS FOODBOOK** in which noted nutritionist Margaret Dean tells you how to manage stress through diet. She offers two complete diets: "The Stress Relief Diet" and "The Stress Prevention Diet". Now you can begin to relieve your tension by strengthening your body.

Use **THE STRESS FOODBOOK** as your personal program for managing stress. Feeling good, you'll be able to use the challenges of stressful situations to your advantage, instead of being overwhelmed by them.

ISBN 87491-089-7/$12.95 hardcover 128 pages, 8 x 9, illustrations

DOMINIQUE'S FAMOUS FISH, GAME & MEAT RECIPES
Classic Dishes Anyone Can Make, Soups, Sauces & Desserts to Go with Them. By Dominique D'Ermo. According to *Gourmet* magazine, Dominique's "landmark restaurant" is "a must for fun, drama, and romance . . . and his menu always has some headline-grabbing dish." Wild Rabbit with Sauce Piquante, Squirrel Poivrade, Rattlesnake Matelote, Marinated Moose Steak, Bear Chops . .

these are but a few of the 200 delicious and unusual recipes for game, fish, meat and everything that goes with them—from sauces to soups and desserts.
ISBN 87491-080-3/$8.95 quality paper
ISBN 87491-082-X/$19.95
limited edttion

COMPLETE GOURMET NUTRITION COOKBOOK, THE
By Margaret Dean, M.S., R.D. Ranked #1 Diet Book by a leading consumer rating service, this book puts the complex findings of the U.S. Senate Dietary Goals into 581 delicious and easy-to-prepare recipes and menus, with good nutritional advice too. The American Library Association's Booklist says, "An excellent introduction to human nutrition."
ISBN 87491-215-6/$16.95 hardcover

Are There Acropolis Books
You Want But Cannot Find In Your Local Stores?

You can get any Acropolis book title in print. Simply send title and retail price, plus $.50 per copy to cover mailing and handling costs for each book desired. District of Columbia residents add applicable sales tax. Enclose check or money order only, no cash please, to: ACROPOLIS BOOKS LTD., 2400 17th ST., NW, WASHINGTON, D.C. 20009. OR SEND FOR OUR COMPLETE CATALOGUE OF ACROPOLIS BOOKS.

Follow Your Horoscope to a Slimmer You

DIET SIGNS

Diet Signs is the first astrological guide to weight loss. It's a book for anyone who has tried to lose weight and failed, time and again. Now you can lose weight, stick to a diet and do it simply, easily and healthfully—and it's all done with astrology.

The secret is timing. For centuries astrologers and farmers have known that the sun affects the plumpness of fruits and vegetables; but now noted astrologer, Joanne Lemieux, proves that it also affects the weight of people. She has charted the weight gain and weight loss cycles for each sun sign—an invaluable secret to anyone struggling with a diet. Because now if you know your sign, you'll know exactly when you can lose the most weight with the least effort.

In **Diet Signs** you'll also learn what specific days of the year it is almost impossible for you to lose weight, no matter how hard you try. "Just realize," says Ms. Lemieux, "that during the times you find it hardest to diet you are coming under cosmic stress, but it will not last for long." Either don't bother to diet at these times (just relax and wait) or be assured that you'll see the dramatic weight loss you want right after those "bad days."

When you are ready to reduce, you'll find the perfect diet for your sun sign here—complete with menus and recipes for many dishes. Your sign-tailored diet takes into account what you like to do and the foods you like to eat. For instance, Sagittarians, who are travelers, get a wide variety of "exotic" dishes, like "Mexican Chicken" and strawberries in champagne. Pisceans' weight, to go with their water sign, tends to fluctuate a great deal, due to water retention. Pisceans are warned to decrease their salt intake. Their diet includes many liquids like soups and special drinks as well as seafood.

Along with dieting, Ms. Lemieux believes that exercise is vital to keep you healthy. She has determined, therefore, which type of exercise will most satisfy and slim each sun sign. For instance, Aries people like people, so they are advised to take up a team sport. Geminis, who hate hard physical labor, should play golf or join a bicycle club.

Diet Signs is your complete guide to successful weight loss "in tune with the stars."

About the author

Joanne Lemieux is an astrologer and active member of the Astrological Association of Northern Virginia. She is a moon child whose interest in this book came from her own lifetime of dieting. She is an avid cook, and is the daughter of a nurse and is a former nursing student herself. Ms. Lemieux has written a children's book and a monthly astrology column.